More Seen, Un-Seen Disneyland

An Un-Official, Un-Authorized Look at What You See at Disneyland, but Never Really See

Russell D. Flores

2015
CyberForce, U.S.A.

More Seen, Un-Seen Disneyland: An Un-Official, Un-Authorized Look at What You See at Disneyland, but Never Really See.
By Russell D. Flores

Published by
CyberForce
7405 Greenback Suite 444
Citrus Heights, CA 95610
www.sudbooks.com

All rights reserved. No part of this book may be reproduced or transmitted in any form or by any means, either electronic or mechanical, including photocopying, recording, photographs, or by any information storage or retrieval system without written permission from the author or their publisher.

All photography by
Russell Flores

Written by
Russell D. Flores

ISBN: 978-0-9646293-3-2

© Copyright 2015

First Edition

10 9 8 7 6 5 4 3 2 1

Printed in the United States of America

Cover Picture: The cover picture was taken by the author. Seven people were removed from the picture and the author and his wife were added.

DISCLAIMERS

Disney Disclaimer: Disneyland, Disney, all attraction names, names of lands, Character names, landmarks, etc referenced in this book are the Copyright © and/or Trademarks ® of The Walt Disney Company or their appropriate subsidiary or affiliate. This publication is in no way authorized by, endorsed by or affiliated with The Walt Disney Company, The Disneyland Resort nor any of their subsidiaries or affiliates. All references to any and all Walt Disney Company Copyrights © / Trademark ® or subsidiary company or affiliated company's Copyrights ©/Trademark ® are used in accordance with the Fair Use Doctrine and are not meant to imply this publication is a Walt Disney Company, Disneyland Resort, Disney subsidiary, Disney Affiliate, etc., product for any advertising or commercial purpose.

Walt Disney Family Museum Disclaimer: The Walt Disney Family Museum, all attraction names, items in their collection, etc referenced in this book are the Copyright © and/or Trademarks ® of Walt Disney Family Museum, The Disney Family, or the appropriate person loaning the item. This publication is in no way authorized by, endorsed by or affiliated with the Walt Disney Family Museum, The Walt Disney Family Foundation, The Disney Family nor any other person(s) associated with the museum. All references to any and all Walt Disney Family Museum Copyrights © / Trademark ® are used in accordance with the Fair Use Doctrine and are not meant to imply this publication is a Walt Disney Family Museum, Disney Family, or other person(s) affiliated with the museum, etc., product for any advertising or commercial purpose.

Lucas Disclaimer: THX-1138, Star Wars, C-3PO, R2-D2, X-Wing, Indiana Jones, etc referenced in this book are the Copyright © / Trademarks ® of George Lucas, Lucas Films, Ltd., or its subsidiaries or affiliates. This publication is in no way authorized by, endorsed by or affiliated with the George Lucas, Lucas Films, Ltd., nor any of their subsidiaries or affiliates. All references to any and all George Lucas, Lucas Films, Ltd., Subsidiaries or affiliates' Copyright ©/Trademark ® are used in accordance with the Fair Use Doctrine and are not meant to imply this publication is a George Lucas, Lucas Films, Ltd., nor any subsidiary or affiliate, etc., product for any advertising or commercial purpose.

General Disclaimer: Any reference to any Copyright © / Trademark ® on Disney property are the property of their respective owners. This publication is in no way authorized by, endorsed by or affiliated with and of these owners nor any of their subsidiaries or affiliates. All references to any Copyright © / Trademark ® or affiliated company's Copyright © / Trademark ® are used in accordance with the Fair Use Doctrine and are not meant to imply this publication is a any way one of these companies, product for any advertising or commercial purpose.

DISCLAIMERS CONTINUED

Accuracy Disclaimer: While I have attempted to make every reasonable effort and precaution in the making of this publication to ensure its accuracy, the Publisher and Author assume no responsibility for errors or omissions. Neither is any liability assumed for damages resulting, or alleged to result, either directly or indirectly from the use of the information contain in this publication.

Photograph Disclaimer: Every photograph was taken at Disneyland and is a true representation of what the photographer saw with the following exceptions. Some Guests' and Cast Members' faces have been blurred or they have been photo edited out of the picture to protect their identity and /or their presence in the picture was distracting. Color enhancement, photo sharpening, distracting artifact removal, and cropping were used to make some photos more presentable and to fit the book's format. Some pictures are a composite or montage of several pictures.

Disneyland is always trying to Plus (DL) their attractions (DL). Because of the nature of this book, the book could not possibly keep up with all of the changes. Many items may be moved occasionally such as the sea shells setup in the shape of Mickey's head on the Pirate of the Caribbean. Look around to see if you can find it. Unfortunately some things may be removed, but rest assured that the Disney Imagineers (DL) have replaced it with another wonderful item.

This book is not an official Disney publication. It is not done in association with or endorsed by The Walt Disney Company, Disneyland, The Disneyland Resort, or any of its affiliates or subsidiaries.

All references to or photographs of any and all Walt Disney Company Copyright © / Trademark ®, and subsidiary company's or affiliated company's Copyrights / Trademark ®, or any other company's Copyright © / Trademark ® material are used in accordance with the Fair Use Doctrine and are not meant to imply this publication of The Walt Disney Company, Disneyland, Disneyland Resort, Disney subsidiary, Disney Affiliate, or any other company, etc., unless stated.

The opinions of expressed in this book are those of the author and are not necessarily those of The Walt Disney Company, its affiliates or subsidiaries. This book is meant as a travel guide and work of commentary.

AUTHOR'S NOTES

Throughout the book, you will see (EN:YY), the YY being a number. This indicates that there is a note. If you are interested, go to the notes chapter at the back of the book and see the indicated number.

When you see (DL) following a word, it stands for "Disney Language." This is a word or phrase that is used in the Disney community. If you are unfamiliar with the word, go to the Disney Language section at the back of the book for a short definition.

TABLE OF CONTENTS

Title Page	1
Copyright Page	2
Disclaimers	3
Author's Notes	
Table of Contents	5
Acknowledgements	6
Dedication	7
Foreword	8
Introduction	9
1. Now Arriving, In More Seen, Un-Seen Disneyland, The Disneyland Railroad. 'BOARD!	16
2. Urban Legends: I heard from a friend, who heard from…	32
3. Disneyland Pays Tributes	59
4. OK, A Few More Hidden Mickeys	75
5. I Think I've Seen That Before?	87
6. I'm Still Not Bad, I'm Still Just Drawn That Way	98
7. What is that doing there?	105
8. Sounds? In a picture book? That's Just Crazy Talk!	114
9. Gone but Still There: Or, More Ghost of Disneyland Attractions Past	130
10. What's in a name?	149
11. More Signs or Signs, Signs, Man, They Are Everywhere	158
12. It's Just Landscaping, Isn't it?	174
13. We Already Know Everything about the Haunted Mansion, Don't We?	182
14 WOW, That's Interesting!	197
About the Author	233
Internet Links to the Seen, Un-Seen Series	234
End Notes	235
Bibliography	259
Disney Language	267

ACKNOWLEDGEMENTS

I would like to take this time to thank all of the people who supported me in this endeavor.

All of the Disney authors, bloggers, photographers, and podcasters whose material proved invaluable in my research.

All of the great podcasts and web pages that have promoted my work.

Dave Smith, Bob Gurr, Alice Davis, Jeff Kurtti, Rolly & Marie Crump, Tony Baxter, Kevin Kidney, David Koenig, Jeff Heimbuch, George Taylor, Jeff Baham, Tim O'Day, Nik Ranieri, Kevin Kidney and Jody Daily (Kevin & Jody), Sam Gennawey, Michael Campbell, Michael Broggie, David Lesjak, Paul Barrie, Michael Bowling, Ken Pellman, Randy Crane, Paul Sorokoski, Bill Barbe; Todd Pierce, Don Peri, Chris Strodder, and T. Lewis who were so kind in answering all of my emails and / or questions.

To my proof reader, subject matter expert, and friend Jeff Heimbuch.

Don Hahn for giving me a little push at a critical point in this project.

My reviewers Dave Smith, David Koenig, Bob Gurr, Don Hahn, Tom and Tony Bancroft (The Bancroft Brothers), Bill Cotter, and George Taylor for their invaluable feedback.

Bob Gurr for taking so much of his valuable time to answer my questions, track down an answer for me, review my book, and for writing the forward.

A special thank you to Dave Smith for answering so many questions, his encouragement, review of this book, and providing the first comment again for the back of my book.

My friends Liana Killgore, Chris Allison, Thomas (Tommy Pix) Allison, Lynn Yaw, Jon & Bess Ament, Tim & Jane Jinks, Lynn Barron, Kaitlin Gee, Jenna Haskins, Arthur Vasser, Matt Bell, Wendy Cooper, Alan Hooper, Don Morin, David Smith, HW, and Keith Gluck whose encouragement was so helpful.

I would like to add another special thank you to my confidential consultants who helped me work through a last minute problem with my book. You know who you are.

To anyone who may have slipped through the cracks on the thank yous.

And last, but definitely not least, I would like to thank my family for all their love and support.

DEDICATION

This book is simply dedicated to the two biggest loves in my life, my wife and daughter.

FOREWORD

You have in your hands a visual treat - a photographic explanation of what Walt Disney taught all of us early Imagineers about visual thoroughness. About why something seems right, even though we don't know why. The explanation, in words, was what John Hench was so good at. All knowledgeable Disneyland fans know exactly who John Hench was; Walt's go-to man for endlessly teaching his awareness of details, not just to those of us just starting out in 1954 to design Disneyland, but to every generation of new Imagineers. Why? As it has been said many times, "It's in the details."

From the perspective of every person Walt gathered up into his WED Enterprises, I doubt that most of us gave much thought to "the details". But Walt sure did. Eventually, we all caught on to why. On page 78 in <u>Designing Disney</u> by John Hench, readers will learn a quick lesson in details, and how they are essential in telling thorough and believable tales, whether movie or Disneyland attraction. It's all the same; too little and too much detail ruins the story's believability. John goes on to explain the human mind, the visual cues that are registered unconsciously, the whole that is due to the details. We see…but never see.

So dear reader, you think you know Disneyland? You think you've seen everything? Well, you're in for a treat. You'll find yourself dragging this wonderful edition with you on every future visit, becoming dog-eared with notations as you search ever deeper into our land…Disneyland. You'll find the most delightful visual treasures. You'll understand why other places you may visit leave an undefined discomfort. You'll recognize why: the ever important details are missing. Believe me, you'll become as expert as any Imagineer in understanding, "It's in the details."

Bob Gurr
Former Imagineer

INTRODUCTION

"We were redoing the Storybook Land attraction and trying to cut its budget. One of the art directors said, 'Walt, we can just use regular glass rather than stained.' Walt said something profound, 'Look, the thing that's going to make Disneyland unique and different is the detail. If we lose the detail, we lose it all.'"

Dick Nunis, Disneyland Theme Park Executive (EN: 8)

In my first book, I used the introduction to explain why I had written the book. In this introduction, I would like to spend my time explaining why I think Walt Disney, and now The Walt Disney Company, took the time to add all of these wonderful details. In my first book, I talked about the story of Walt Disney and the construction worker who was working on the Storybook Land Canal Boats during its construction. The worker asked Walt Disney why he was bothering to put so much extra detail, and added cost, when no one would know. Walt Disney famously answered, "I'll know", and then went on to explain the importance of detail.

What did Walt Disney mean with his answer? And why has Disneyland, Walt Disney Imagineering, and The Walt Disney Company as a whole, continue to put all these extra details into the attractions? I don't think Walt Disney literally meant that he would know. I think he was speaking in broader terms. In the movie business, when filming a scene, it is important for the background to be as complete as possible, but not so much that it is distracting. If you are filming a scene that is supposed to be taking place at a train station, then you need visual and audio elements so people will know where the scene is taking place and believe the action is real. Too much detail and the camera doesn't see it anyway. If there are too few details people will be confused. Or worse than that, realize they are watching a movie. If you stop and look at a scene in a movie, you may notice many elements you never realized were there. Many people do this for fun now to see what little "EASTER EGGS" the director and / or the film crew have placed into scenes. In *Saving Mr. Banks*, there are several of these in the scenes that take place in Walt Disney's office. Did you notice the tributes to Walt Disney World and Rolly Crump?

It is more than that, though. The mind is a wonderfully complicated thing. Even though you may not be completely conscious of every detail in the scene, your mind's eye is. It all helps to make the scene more believable. These details make your mind actually believe the scene is taking place where the movie says it is.

As an example, if there was a kitchen scene, but the set decorator used office furniture, you would immediately be taken out of the movie and start to wonder what was going on. You wouldn't be paying attention to the action, but wondering why is there office furniture in the kitchen.

Now let's take that same scene, but this time have a kitchen table and a stove. Your mind will now accept that the scene could be taking place. You wouldn't be pulled out of the movie by the wrong context being shown. That is good, but could they make the scene better? Of course they can. They can add cabinets, a counter, refrigerator, hanging cooking utensils, art work from their children on the refrigerator, a collection of salt and pepper shakers on top of the cabinets, dirty dishes in the sink, and a garbage can. Are all of these details necessary to make you believe you are in a kitchen? As I said before, no. Are you actually conscious of all of these details? Probably not. Does it draw you deeper into believing the movie scene is real? Absolutely, yes. Your mind picks up on all these details, making it more comfortable with the scene and therefore more likely to be drawn deeper into the "reality" of the situation, and the movie as a whole. I know that there are stage plays that feature minimal or no backgrounds. The audience is supposed to imagine the visual elements. This is an extreme in the other direction and requires great acting on the part of the performers to make the scenes believable.

"When Fred Moore started animating the dwarfs, Walt made him do it over and over. He'd pick a finger, the way Grumpy's eye worked and the little details. It wasn't so much that he was picking on Fred, he was sharing the experience with Fred."

Frank Thomas, Disney Animator. (EN: 9)

Walt Disney famously coined the term "Plus" (DL) during the 1940's. (EN: 1) This obviously means the idea didn't start with Disneyland. Even though the term originated in the 1940's, this idea goes even back further in Disney history. Walt Disney was always looking for ways to make his projects better. Even after a project started, he would still look for ways to improve them. Walt would scrap work already done on scenes and start them over if he believed they could be made better. When Walt went from black and white to color or from silent to talkies, he did so in order to improve his products. He saw technology as a way to add more details. He wanted his films to be more believable. Walt didn't just hire animators and put them to work, as most studios did. He sent them to classes. He didn't just use existing technology. He was always looking for something better, something new, something innovative. Walt wasn't satisfied with early sound technology. He strived to produce films with better sound quality. Even when he found and started using a new sound system or color film, he still continued to look for better ones.

Walt Disney didn't just look for technologies to make his films better, he also helped create them. If the technology he needed to Plus his film didn't exist, he would have his people try and come up with a way to accomplish what he wanted done. The Multiplane Camera (DL), used by the Disney Studios and invented by Bill Garity and his staff, is one example. (EN: 270) Walt wanted a way to give depth and dimension to his cartoons. This was not possible with the single plane of existing camera systems. The new Multiplane Camera allowed the film crew to place each visual plane of the scene on its own plane. This in turn allowed for each plane to be spaced appropriately and moved independently of each other. As you walk down a road, things closer appear to move faster than objects farther away. This new camera system allowed the film makers to make this detail a visually possible in their films. Even though Walt Disney didn't invent the idea of making a film with a 360 degree view, he made the product better with another Ub Iwerks invention that used multiple cameras tied together in a new and innovative way.

Many people felt all the extra details Walt Disney added to his films and attractions were a waste of time and money. Imagineer Marc Davis told Walt one day that people wouldn't even notice all the work put into the auctioneer pirate in Pirates of the Caribbean. At the time, the auctioneer was the cutting edge in Audio-Animatronics (DL). Walt told Marc that the extra detail wouldn't go unnoticed. Disney said the auctioneer would be part of the reason people would want to ride the attraction over and over again. And when they did, each time they would notice something new. (EN: 2) Walt Disney knew from experience with Plussing his movies that people, even if not consciously aware of it, loved the quality of them. They wanted to see them again and again. He wanted the same for Disneyland.

Walt Disney did not leave it up to his construction workers to tell him what was going on. He wandered through the Park. He would look at the plans, and if he didn't know how to read something, he would learn. (EN: 10 / 308) He even went so far as to kneel down during construction to get a kid's eye view of the park. He wanted everything to look right from every Guest's point of view. No one ever considered what a child would see that could take them out of the experience. But, Walt Disney did. (EN: 5)

In my first book, I wrote about a garbage can that directed my attention to all the extra details that had been put into Disneyland. That's probably why I found this story in "Walt Disney: An American Original", by Bob Thomas so fascinating.

"During the planning and construction of Disneyland, Walt Disney and all the WED employees were working 48 hour weeks. They often went to lunch together and Walt Disney would inspire his employees with his ideas and goals. He would talk about how he wanted his concepts implemented down to every detail. He even talked about those trash cans. He wanted them to not just be 'utilitarian eyesores', but to look like they belonged where they were." (EN: 7)

Just like his movies, Walt Disney wanted his Disneyland Guests to be immersed in the experience. Everything needed to belong in the "scene". One land needed to blend into the next, but by the same token, Guests needed to know they had moved from one land to the next. This transition is just like in a movie where one scene slowly fades into another. (EN: 11) When you combine all of this together, it is the concept of "Architecture of Reassurance". Everything you see looks like it belongs, or in other terms, there are no contradictions. Your minds relaxes because you are led to believe everything is "right". This helps you to feel comfortable. This was very important to Walt Disney. (EN:86) He once reprimanded a publicity man for parking his car near the original Frontierland train station. Walt Disney was upset because a car didn't belong on the frontier. The man was taking the Guests out of the experience, just like the office furniture would have done in my kitchen example. (EN: 4) Walt Disney even went so far as to not use the design for a building because he felt the designer was trying to build as a monument to himself. Walt wanted all designs to be done for an enjoyable experience. Walt Disney reportedly said, "All I want you to think about is that when people walk through or ride through or have access to anything that you design, I want them, when they leave, to have smiles on their faces. Just remember that; it's all I ask of you as a designer." (EN: 6)

This does lead to the question: why is there a medieval castle at the end of a turn-of-the-century main street? Should this detail pull us out of our experience? Yes and no. It is a contradiction. But done right, a contradiction like this is more of a curiosity. It makes you wonder what is it doing there, and draws you in deeper. This is what Walt Disney referred to as a Weenie (DL). There is a famous story about how Walt Disney would get home late and, not wanting to wake his family, would quietly make a hot dog (or weenie) for himself. He noticed that the weenie always got their dog's attention. I know the concept of having something to get someone's attention wasn't new to Walt Disney, but this incident gave Walt a name for it. (EN: 271)

The entrance to each land has a Weenie to draw people into it. The Castle initially draws people deeper into the Park. Once they are in the central hub, it then does double duty and serves as the Weenie for Fantasyland. The Enchanted Tiki Room and bamboo arch serves as the Weenie for Adventureland just as the Cavalry Fort entrance serves that purpose for Frontierland. In the past, the People Mover drew people into Tomorrowland. That function has now been given to the Astro Orbitor. The concept of the Weenie was also use to draw people into various parts of the Park, including into attractions. Walt Disney didn't simply put a sign up saying "Such and Such Land". He Plussed it with these Weenies to inspire and sense of curiosity in Guests to go deeper into different areas of the Park.

The Plussing didn't stop with the completion of the Park in 1955. Walt Disney was always looking for ways to continue to Plus Disneyland. (EN: 3) Several things, such as Tomorrowland, were not completed when Disneyland first opened. Walt put his attention to not only those, but to other ways to make the Park a better experience. Although in typical Walt Disney fashion, he did not let the bad publicity from opening day problems, better known as "Black Sunday", get him down. However, he did take note of it (EN:121). Just three short years after the opening of Disneyland, the Park underwent the first major re-furbishment (referred to in Disney Language as a re-furb (DL)) with additions to Tomorrowland. Just as people are sad today to see an attraction make way for a new one, I'm sure people were upset when Walt Disney removed several attractions to make way for the Submarines, Matterhorn, Monorail, People Mover, new Autopia tracks and vehicles, and new location for Rocket Jets. And the addition of details continued too. Walt Disney didn't just add a bunch of new things all sitting next to each other. These additions were intertwined with each other to form a harmonious blend of sets and motion. The Monorail wasn't just a box hung in the sky, but a themed, modern vehicle which looked like it could have just arrived from space. The People Mover doors didn't just simply open; the roof tilted to help people load and unload quicker and to prevent them from bumping their heads.

No detail was overlooked by Walt Disney. One day in a meeting, someone brought up the character costumes. Another person said that Walt didn't want to be bothered by costumes. Walt Disney responded, "Wait a minute, They're probably the most important part of the Park." (EN: 12) He recognized that just having his characters in his Park wasn't what made him different; it was the quality of those characters that would keep people coming back.

The Walt Disney Company has strayed a couple of times in the past from this detail driven, Plus-Minded idea, but that has never proved to be a money saver or maker. These little cuts were always quickly noticed by Guests. So why does The Walt Disney Company strive to make things the best? Why do they keep adding details? Some people will say this is the "What would Walt do?" philosophy. That is part of it, but it goes deeper than that. Here is what Walt Disney had to say about this philosophy:

"I think by this time my staff, my young group of executives, and everyone else are convinced that Walt was right. The quality will out (sic). And so I think they're going to stay with that policy because it's proved that it's a good business policy. Give the people everything you can give them. Keep the place as clean as you can keep it. Keep it friendly, you know. Make it a real fun place to be. I think they're convinced and I think they'll bang on…if…as you say…well, after Disney."

Walt Disney (EN: 13)

Much time has passed, and yet, in a way, very little time has passed since Walt Disney's untimely death. Many books, newspaper articles, magazine stories, videos, and even movies have been made since Walt Disney's passing. Some are outstanding and some are questionable. The wonderful Walt Disney Family Museum was created and built at the direction of his daughter, the late Diane Disney Miller. This museum was built with the intent of documenting the man and to remind people that Walt Disney wasn't just a commercial icon. With all of this information about Walt Disney and his legacy, you would think identifying why Walt Disney placed so much emphasis on detail would be a simple matter. But like the man, all of these sources just make it more complex to identify why, and yet also point to the reason. After much reading, talking to other Disney experts and fans, and a lot of thinking on the subject, I have come to the conclusion that the answer is simple: we are the reason that Walt Disney included so much detail in all of his products. His attitude of always giving the audience the best you can do makes the details absolutely necessary. Walt Disney never wanted to produce something that was "good enough." He didn't always attain what he would have considered the best, but with the constraints placed on him by time, money, and technology, he always did his best. And that is one of the key hallmarks of this great man.

To me, Walt Disney was an artist, a visionary, a tinkerer, a businessman, driven, a humanitarian, a husband, and a father. But most of all, Walt Disney was a human, who understood what people wanted and gave them the best. He is Uncle Walt.

So let's take a look at some of these wonderful details that make's Walt Disney's Park so special.

Now Arriving, In

More Seen, Un-Seen Disneyland, The Disneyland Railroad.
'BOARD!

> "For him, the main attraction at Disneyland was the steam trains. Walt needed them for transportation and wanted them for everyone to enjoy."
>
> **Ollie Johnston** (EN: 195)

One of the first attractions Walt Disney wanted to build for Disneyland was the Disneyland Railroad (DLRR). He actually built it with his own money, and his personal holding company Walt Disney, Inc.. The name was later changed to RETLAW, which owned it until 1982.(EN: 18) The name RETLAW comes from Walter spelled backwards. All of the Cast Members for the DLRR worked directly for Walt Disney and received their pay checks from RETLAW. Their checks were reportedly signed by him, but that would be a lot of checks to sign and is probably just an urban legend. (EN: 17 / 130 / 284)

The Santa Fe Railroad agreed to be the sponsor for this attraction. On opening day, the attraction was called the Santa Fe & Disneyland Railroad. Santa Fe maintained their sponsorship until 1974, at which time the name was shortened to the Disneyland Railroad. (EN: 16)

There were only two engines the first day. The two engines were named the C. K. Holliday and E. P. Ripley, former Santa Fe Railroad executives.

Most people don't realize that these two engines were built from scratch at the Walt Disney Studios' machine shop. These two engines cost about $100,000 to build. (EN: 14) Both engines' were inspired by Walt Disney's personal miniature steam engine, the Lilly Belle, but each has its own unique design. Engine #1's design is based on a typical 1870 freight train and was given a classic diamond smoke stack. Engine #2's design is based on passenger engines and was given a more elegant straight smoke stack. (EN: 131) The train track is narrow gauge and has a 3 foot span from rail to rail. Both engines are 5/8th scale, with a 7/8th scale cab to accommodate crew members. (EN: 20)

LEFT: This is a modern copy of the patch worn by the engine crews when the Park first opened and was known as the Santa Fe & Disneyland Railroad. (EN: 19)

The shape of the smoke stacks are based on the type of fuel the engine burn in real world operations. Diamonds were used for wood burning and straight were used for coal. Disneyland uses bio-diesel fuel so the shapes are just for decorative purposes. (EN: 285)

LEFT: Engine #1, the C. K. Holliday, named for the founder of the Santa Fe Railroad.

BELOW: Engine #2, the E. P. Ripley, named for the First President of the Santa Fe Railroad after its reorganization in 1895. (EN: 132)

ABOVE AND BELOW: On March 28, 1958, Engine #3, the Fred Gurley (named for the President of the Santa Fe Railroad 1944 - 1957) was added. (EN: 281) This time, though, a vintage Baldwin engine was purchased and re-furbished at a cost of about $37,061. (EN: 15) This was the first Disneyland Railroad engine not built from scratch. (EN: 78)

The next two engines were also purchased and re-furbished. Engine #4, the Ernest S. Marsh, was named for the President of the Santa Fe Railroad (1957 to 1966). It was added July 25, 1959. (EN: 143 / 282)

Engine #5, the Ward Kimball, was added June 25, 2005. The Ward Kimball engine is named for the famous Disney Studio artist and WED Imagineer. Ward was a big train enthusiast, much like Walt Disney. There is a famous story about Walt and Ward attending the 1948 Railroad Fair in Chicago and visiting the "Henry Ford Museum and Greenfield Village" in Dearborn, MI. These two locations were seeds for the birth of Disneyland. (EN:23)

LEFT: Engine #4, the Ernest S. Marsh.

RIGHT: Engine #5, the Ward Kimball.

Originally, there were only two train stations: The Main Street Station and the Frontierland Station (now known as the New Orleans Square / Frontierland Station). Each train would make a complete circle around Disneyland and only loaded / unloaded at their assigned station. The C.K. Holliday freight train used the Frontierland Station and the E. P. Ripley passenger train used the Main Street Station. While one train was loading / unloading, the other train would make the loop around the Park. This meant a siding or passing track was needed at each station. Although not connected with switches anymore, you can still see the passing track at the Main Street Station and where the tracks were located at the New Orleans Square / Frontierland Station. (EN: 42)

On July 18th, 1955, the first, and only, mishap with the train occurred. The brakeman threw the switch at the Main Street Station before the rear trucks of the caboose had transferred to the passing track. The train continued forward, pulling the front half of the caboose down the passing track and the rear part down the main line. As the caboose pivoted, its rear turned out and struck the concrete of the station before hitting the other train. The caboose derailed. No one was hurt and the caboose was put back on the track that night with a crane. New procedures were put in place to prevent this from happening again. The system operated this way until Spring of 1958, when Engine #3, the Fred Gurley, was added and a new system had to be utilized. The more traditional train system of dividing the tracks into sections and controlling the trains with red / green lights was used. (EN: 43)

ABOVE AND RIGHT: At the Main Street Station, you can see the passing spur just past the main line. This track is only used for holding the handcar and for theming.

ABOVE: Today, the Main Street Station siding is the home of the Disneyland Handcar. The handcar can occasionally be seen on the main line, but not very often. The one time I saw the handcar on the main line, a Cast Member told me that they were riding it out to get an item a Guest had dropped. It is sometimes removed for appearances at train events.

BELOW: Have you ever wondered why there is a large rock covered area in front of the New Orleans Square / Frontierland Train station? Although the tracks for the Frontierland station siding have been removed, this is the area where the siding used to be. (EN: 269)

ABOVE: If you look at the building to the left, you will notice that it appears to have an angled curb. This was to accommodate the siding. The additional paving was added after the removal of the spur. (EN: 283)

BELOW: You may be wondering how the trains were able to pass each other, with the station and water tower on the far side of the tracks. Prior to 1962, the train station and water tower were on the near side of the tracks. In 1962, they were moved to the opposite side as part of the New Orleans Square addition. The tunnel was also built as part of Haunted Mansion's construction. (EN: 41)

When Disneyland first opened, all of the wheels on the original train cars had the word "Disneyland" on them in raised lettering. As they would wear out beyond being re-furbished, they would be replaced. At an unknown point in time, they began using wheels with engraved lettering, which is the style still in use today.

ABOVE: The old style wheels with raised lettering. These wheels have been retired and were donated to Walt's Barn, which is located in Griffith Park, Los Angeles. (EN:138)

BELOW: The new engraved wheels. Sometimes they are covered with oil and dirt, which can make it look like they don't have any writing on them.

ABOVE: If you look at the sides of the wheel trucks on some of the trains, you will see a cap called a bolster cover. You will notice that they have the classic raised lettering "Disneyland Railroad", and this one is actually dated 1955. The railroad was actually named Santa Fe & Disneyland Railroad in 1955, so this bolster cover was actually made at least 20 years later. Also note the serial number was never engraved. Since these parts do not actually rub against anything, they last much longer and could have been placed into service anytime in the last 40 years. So why do trains have bolster covers? The bolster cover is used to access parts of the truck that need periodic lubrication.

(EN: 139 / 276)

ABOVE: A closer look at the writing on the bolster cover.

25

You may also notice numbers on the ground by the tracks as you travel around the Park. You may think they are distance markers, but they are markers for the track segments, put into operation when the system was converted from the passing train system. For safety purposes, the track is divided into 11 blocks. No two trains are allowed to be in the same block at the same time. As an engine enters a block, the light for that section turns red, signaling the following train to not enter until that block is clear. (EN: 21)

ABOVE: The Block 1 marker can be seen on the left side of the train as it leaves the Main Street Station.

RIGHT: The Block 2 marker can be found while passing behind The Jungle Cruise, on the left side.

BOTTOM LEFT: The Block 5 marker can be seen on the right side of the train just as you enter the tunnel before the Toontown Station.

RIGHT: The Block 9 marker is on the right side of the train, just before you enter the tunnel for the Grand Canyon.

Next time you are on the train, see if you can find all 11.

The Engineers always seem to place the engine in the perfect location to allow Guests to board, and to allow for the lift to be perfectly lowered into place for Guests needing special assistance. You may think they operate the train so much they know exactly where to stop, but you'd only be partially correct. There are three different engine lengths. So how does the Engineer know the correct spot to stop? If you look on the right side of the engines after it stops at each station, you will notice some small poles with numbers on them. These numbers correspond to the engine's length and tell the Engineers where to stop the engine so the cars line up correctly with the station. (EN: 277)

LEFT: These markers are located at the New Orleans Square/ Frontierland Station.

BELOW: These markers are at the Tomorrowland Station.

LEFT: These markers are at the Toontown Station and can be seen just behind the it's a small world facade.

Have you ever seen the wig wag crossing signals just after passing it's a small world? They were donated to the park by the Santa Fe Railroad. Originally, they wanted to donate an actual railroad crossing signal, but it would have been out of proportion to the Disneyland Railroad, so Walt Disney politely declined. The Santa Fe San Bernardino shop then built a smaller version of the crossing signals that operated on

windshield wiper motors. The donation was accepted and installed on this road. The train actually crosses several roads on its trip around Disneyland. However, only three actually allow vehicles to cross the tracks; the rest go underneath it in tunnels. In addition to this crossing, there is one located just after you leave the Tomorrowland Station, and one just before the tunnel to the Toontown Station. This one is used to access Big Thunder Ranch. (EN: 22)

LEFT AND BELOW: This crossing signal protects parades and other traffic as the train passes. This is also where the switch that
allows the trains to back into the roundhouse
is located. The roundhouse is backstage (DL).

QUIZ: Can you name these roads?
(Answer EN:24)

ABOVE: Some of the engines have special "Tender Seats" installed in them. Engines 1, 2, and 4 currently have seating installed. Riding in the "Tender Seat" gives you a real feel for what it is like to work on a steam locomotive. The seats only hold 2 to 3 based on Guest size. If you happen to luck out and Disneyland is operating one of the engines with a "Tender Scat", ask one of the Main Street Station conductors if they are giving rides that day. Please keep in mind there are many reason they may not be giving rides, such as the Park being too busy, or safety concerns that trip, such as it being too hot or the train needing to conduct a boiler blow off. (EN: 196 / 197 / 198 / 276)

BELOW LEFT: Who knows, you might get lucky and get a ride like we did.

BELOW RIGHT: A unique view of the cars.

As a kid, besides being able to ride a real train, another reason I enjoyed the Disneyland Railroad was I got to see "real" dinosaurs. The Primeval World Diorama has many dinosaurs, including the brontosaurus, raptors, triceratops, pterodactyl, stegosaurus, and tyrannosaurus rex. This diorama is so well done. What makes it even more marvelous as an adult, is to learn that the dinosaurs were first used at the 1964-1965 New York World's Fair before being brought to Disneyland. That's right, they were created for the Ford Magic Skyway. In addition to this diorama, it's a small world, the People Mover concept, Carousel of Progress, and Great Moments with Mr. Lincoln all debuted at the World's Fair, before coming to Disneyland. (EN: 199 / 200 / 201 / 202 / 301)

ABOVE: Three brontosaurus enjoy a lake and some food.

BELOW LEFT: As you pass a rock monolith, you see 3 pterodactyls. Don't stare too long or...

BELOW RIGHT: ...this guy will startle you being right up against the window.

LEFT: Two triceratops guard their playful young as they hatch. They look like they are smiling to me.

RIGHT: Three peaceful raptors drink from a pond that is almost dried up. They look so peaceful in this scene, but scientist now believe they were carnivores and quite vicious.

BELOW: The final dramatic fight scene between a stegosaurus and a tyrannosaurus rex. When the dinosaur diorama was being developed, Walt Disney insisted that it be as accurate as possible. The problem was that most of the dinosaurs displayed lived millions of years apart. Discussions were held. It was eventually decided that the scenes were so powerful and told a great story, so Walt approved the diorama. (EN: 228) There are other errors based on new scientific discoveries about dinosaurs, such as tyrannosaurus' head being the wrong shape and only having two instead of the three fingers portrayed, and the brontosaurus chewing its food rather than swallowing it whole. (EN: 291 / 292)

URBAN LEGENDS

I heard from a freind, who heard from...

An interesting thing that occurs in society is the development of Urban Legends over time; Disneyland is no exception. Urban Legends can lead to an interesting look into something's past. In some ways, Urban Legends can be thought of as a long term game of "Secret", in which you whisper a secret to one person, they whisper it to another, and so on, until the last person is reached. The last person reveals how the secret has changed. Some Urban Legends are total fabrications or can be hurtful. Some are based on fact but have changed over time, just like the game. Some, however, are true. Let's take a look at several "Urban Legends" (UL) that I find interesting about Disneyland and whether they are TRUE, FALSE, or maybe a little of both.

ABOVE AND BELOW: **UL**-One of the most widely spread Urban Legends is that the hearse in front of Haunted Mansion was used for Brigham Young's funeral.
FALSE: Although it makes for a great story, research into the hearse shows that it was not built until well after Brigham Young's funeral. In addition, Brigham Young was carried by pall bearers, as per his will. Anything with this level of historical significance to any organization would most likely have been purchased by that organization. It is a real hearse and was purchased by Disneyland for use at the Haunted Mansion. The hearse first appeared in front of Haunted Mansion after its 1995 re-furb (DL).
(EN: 25 / 26 / 27 / 28 / 29 / 40)

LEFT: Are you thinking of joining the other 999 ghosts at Haunted Mansion? Be sure to contact the "Ghost Relations Department" for reservations. Note that they do not accept applications in person.

ABOVE: **UL**-Another popular Urban Legend is that all the skeletons in Pirates of the Caribbean are real. Two variations on this are that only the pirate captain or only the skull on the pirate captain's headboard are still real. **TRUE and FALSE**: When Pirates of the Caribbean originally opened, the technology to make realistic skeletons did not exist. The Walt Disney Company obtained a long term loan of several skeletons from UCLA. Several years later, they were able to replace them with realistic artificial skeletons and the originals were returned. The variation legend basically says they were all returned except the pirate captain or the headboard skeleton. A close inspection shows that this is not true. The head and teeth are clearly one piece. If you think about any skeleton you have seen in a science class, you will remember that the skeleton has to be held together with cord or wire. Take a look at the joints in these pictures, or when you are on the attraction, and you will not see anything holding the joints together.
(EN: 31 / 102)

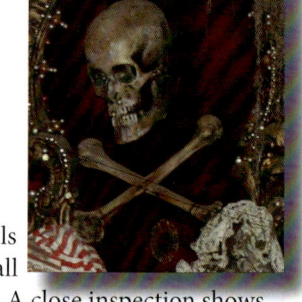

RIGHT: These two guys can be seen in the grotto after the second drop.

LEFT: Just after passing the Captain's Quarters, you'll see the "hidden treasure". This little guy is enjoying all the "pirate booty".

QUIZ: Each of the boats, or Les Bateaux, on Pirates of the Caribbean has a unique name. How many boats are there and what are their names? (Answer EN: 134)

RIGHT: In the pirates' tavern, you see these two pirates playing a perpetual game of chess. But if you could get out and look at the game, you would see they are in a stalemate. (EN: 103)

BELOW: Skeletons can also be found in other attractions, such as Pirate's Lair on Tom Sawyer Island. You have to work to see this guy by turning a crank to lift the him

and the treasure out of the water. You can also find skeletons on such attractions as Indiana Jones Adventure, Jungle Cruise, and of course, Haunted Mansion.

BELOW: This guy can be found in the queue of the Indiana Jones Adventure.

ABOVE AND LEFT: **UL**-The anchor by the Rivers of America is the original anchor from Jean Lafitte's ship. **FALSE**: This anchor has been at the Park since opening day at various locations in Frontierland and New Orleans Square. This legend was actually started by Disneyland and the plaque explains the humor.
(EN: 104 / 109)

RIGHT: **UL**-The carved fish displayed below deck on the Sailing Ship Columbia was carved from a piece of wood from the H.M.S. Bounty, made famous by the book and movie "The Mutiny on the Bounty" fame. **MAYBE TRUE**: Fred Christian, grandson of mutineer Fletcher, reportedly carved it in 1952 from a piece of the H.M.S. Bounty. It was used in a 1978 movie  which used a Bounty replica before being donated to Disneyland. Island inhabitants are known to carve and sell these type of beautiful carving. (EN:100 / 302)

LEFT AND BELOW: **UL**-The beautiful stand in the center of the Enchanted Tiki Room was actually supposed to be a drink service station. **TRUE**: The Enchanted Tiki Room was originally conceived to be a restaurant. The stand was supposed to be the central drink service area for that restaurant. The idea of making the Enchanted Tiki Room a restaurant was changed when it was realized that it would be difficult to keep the Guests moving in and out. Guests could just keep sitting at their tables and watch the show over and over.

It was eventually decided to make the Enchanted Tiki Room a floor show, but not before several items had already been bought for the restaurant. They decided to re-purpose some of these items like the drink service stand. Originally, the Enchanted Tiki Room had individual seats for each Guest. These chairs were originally going to be the chairs for the tables in the restaurant. (EN: 106 / 107 / 265)

UL-The Tiki Room Barker Bird was used to attract Guests to the Tiki Room. He was eventually removed and placed into storage. Several years later, he was re-purposed (DL) and placed at the top of the stairs in the Jungle Cruise queue. Another variation is that the bird in the queue of Pirates of the Caribbean is the original Barker Bird. **FALSE**: I find this Urban Legend very interesting. The Barker Bird was an effective Weenie (DL); in fact, he proved to be too effective. He drew such large crowds that they blocked the entrance to Frontierland. In addition, there were technical problems with the Audio-Animatronic bird being exposed to the elements. After a short time of exposure, his feathers would also become shabby-looking. A special box was used to protect the bird when the Park was closed. There were also several birds used over time. Mainly due to the weather issues, but also because of the crowding problem, the final Barker Bird was removed and sat in storage for many years. In 2014, Disneyland decided to display the Barker Bird in the Disneyana Gallery as part of the Enchanted Tiki Room's 50th anniversary celebration. (EN: 262 / 263 / 293)

BELOW: In 2014, Garner Holt Productions, Inc.™ built a replica of the Barker Bird for the Walt Disney Family Museum that Guests can operate themselves.

LEFT: The bird at the top of the stairs in the Jungle Cruise queue is a Hornbill. He does move and screech to entertain Guests, but alas, he does not talk. (EN: 85)

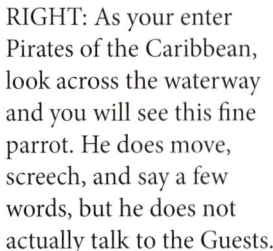

RIGHT: As your enter Pirates of the Caribbean, look across the waterway and you will see this fine parrot. He does move, screech, and say a few words, but he does not actually talk to the Guests.

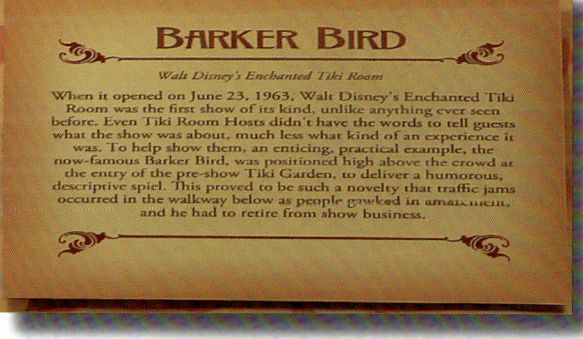

THIS PAGE: One of the real Barker Birds, Juan, was on display in the Disneyana Gallery in 2014 as part of the 50th anniversary celebration for the Enchanted Tiki Room. In spite of the fact that he was not functional, he still attracted many guests. (EN: 266)

An interesting side note about the Barker Bird. He was not originally included in the attraction. He was added later at the suggestion of a Guest.
(EN: 303)

ABOVE AND LEFT: **UL**-There was a bra and corset store at Disneyland on opening day. **TRUE:** Hollywood-Maxwell's Intimate Apparel Shop, commonly referred to as The Wizard of Bras, was an opening day store. It had a full product line and a display of the history of intimate apparel. The Wizard was actually the emcee's voice who told you about the history. This is the only store front with the door and windows raised above street level which was to prevent innocent children's eyes from peeking in. The store only lasted 6 months before closing. (EN: 33 / 99)

BOTTOM: The chairs were provided on the porch for the men to sit, while the ladies went in to shop. (EN: 34)

UL-Guests could buy tobacco and cigarettes at Disneyland.
TRUE: When Disneyland first opened, no one knew the health concerns of tobacco use. Disneyland continued to sell tobacco until 1999. The following year, Disneyland limited the locations that you could smoke tobacco to three places. The Walt Disney Company is very pro-health and anti-tobacco use, and this policy influences all parts of the Company today. (EN: 35)

The use of visual signs goes back to a time when reading was not common. Indians were long associated with tobacco since they introduced Europeans to it. This lead to the use of wooden Indians in front of tobacco stores. The barber pole is another example of a visual sign. (EN: 37)

ABOVE: One of the original tobacco stores was located on Main Street, U.S.A. and was there on opening day. The store is currently used by the 20th Century Music Company, which is located between the Magic Store and the Main Street Cinema. The Indian statue is an exact model used on opening day.

RIGHT: A second tobacco store was in Frontierland and was located in what is now the Westward Ho Trading Company. This Indian statue stood for many years, but was removed in late 2014.

QUIZ: Can you name the three current locations where smoking is allowed inside Disneyland? (Answer EN: 36)

AUTHOR'S NOTE: As with many items at Disneyland, the "wooden indian" may have been replaced with a fiberglass exact replica to protect the original from the elements.

UL- The X-Wing Star Fighter in Star Trader / Starcade is an actual movie prop used in the *Star Wars* © movies. **FALSE:** The X-Wing was actually purposely built for the opening of Star Tours and was housed in the Star Trader. It was eventually moved to the upstairs level of the Starcade, where it hung for many years. The only way for the public to get a look at this beautiful ship was while standing in the outside queue for Space Mountain. When Star Tours was re-furbished in 2011, the X-Wing was again moved back into Star Trader. (EN: 203)

ABOVE: The X-Wing in its current home, hanging in Star Trader.

LEFT: When the X-Wing was moved upstairs in the Starcade, the games were removed from up there and that section was closed to the public and only used for special events. This was the view from the bottom of the escalator for many years.

BELOW: The view of the X-Wing from the Space Mountain queue. Even there, it could be difficult to see due to the sun glare off the windows.

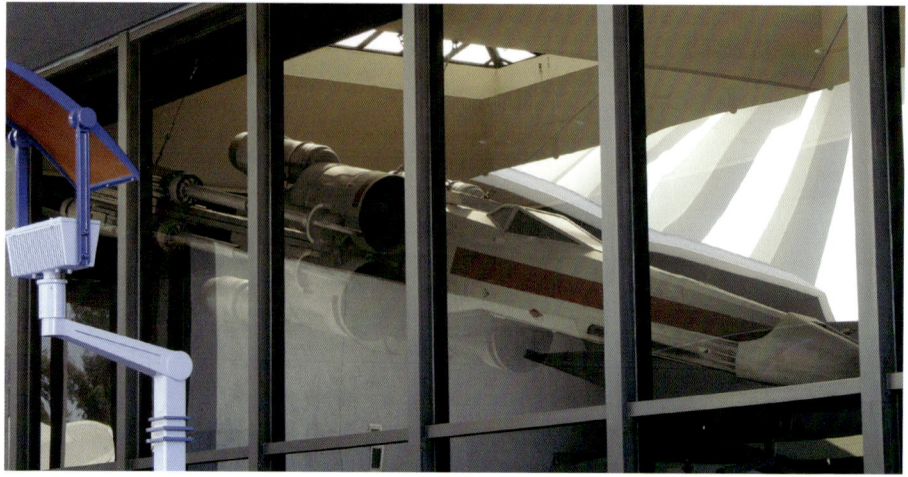

UL-One of my favorite Urban Legends is that the drawbridge on Sleeping Beauty Castle actually works. **FALSE**: The drawbridge actually worked until September 2014, when the chain guard rails were replaced with wooden ones. Prior to that, it was functional and had been raised twice for ceremonial purposes. The first time was on opening day, when the drawbridge was raised before the Park opened and then lowered for the Fantasyland dedication. The drawbridge was again raised in 1983 for the rededication opening ceremony for the newly re-furbished Fantasyland. (EN: 38 / 69)

ABOVE: This picture was taken September 27, 2014 of the Castle with the new bridge. As you can see, there is a new wooden guard railing in place. This railing will not collapse like the previous chain railing, thus preventing the bridge from being raised. In addition, a metal brace was added under the bridge.

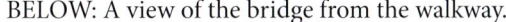

ABOVE: A closer look at the new bridge. In addition to the new railing, you can see a new metal support under the bridge. This support also prevents the bridge from being raised.

BELOW: A view of the bridge from the walkway.

UL-Another Urban Legend about the entrance to Sleeping Beauty Castle is that the gate closes. **FALSE**: Although this would be great, a quick inspection of the gate reveals that this is not true. If you look up at the gate, you will see that it just decoration for the facade. The Imagineers have gone to great lengths to make it appear real, with chains, pulleys, and guides. Beside, how safe would it be to have real spikes hanging over Guests' heads?

BELOW: Standing under the gate, looking up

ABOVE: Front view of the Castle Gate

RIGHT: A close up close picture into the gate's mounts.

BELOW: A closer look at the gate.

PREVIOUS PAGE: A picture of the Castle when the bridge was still functional.

RIGHT: You can see the 2 slots on the front of the Castle where the arms that raise the bridge fit.

LEFT: This photo shows inside the Castle, behind the right arm. You can see the arm goes into the Castle, allowing it to be used as a fulcrum to raise the bridge.

BELOW: A close up of the hinge, which is the pivot point of the fulcrum.

BELOW LEFT AND BELOW RIGHT: As you can see, the wooden bridge is actually not part of the stone bridge.

UL- In 1961, an anonymous donor from Italy sculpted and shipped the Snow White and the Seven Dwarfs statues to Disneyland. Walt loved them and decided to place them in the Park, but they were in the wrong proportions. The Snow White statue was the same height as the dwarfs. Apparently the sculptor had based his proportions on a set of soaps that displayed Snow White as basically the same height of the dwarfs. The problem was solved by John Hench with a little forced perspective and the statues have stood in the current location ever since.

TRUE, FALSE, and MAYBE: The statues you see today are not the original statues. The strong California sun and weather were destroying them, so in order to preserve them, they were moved to the Walt Disney Archives where there are today. Exact duplicates were made from the originals out of a material that could withstand the California weather better and put into their place.

That is only part of the story. Were the statues actually an anonymous gift? During a presentation in September 2011, A Disney Imagineer reportedly told the audience that the story was a wonderful back story (DL) created by Walt Disney Imagineering to explain the size discrepancy. Reportedly after John Hench passed away, his secretary went through his files. She is said to have found a file that indicated the company had ordered the statues. When they received the statues, they discovered the size discrepancy and Hench corresponded with the sculptor to find out how much it would cost to have another Snow White made. The cost was too high so they decided to just come up with their own solution. Of course that solution was forced perspective. The story to explain the size discrepancy was created, and John Hench even told the story in his book, *Designing Disney*. Later when Imagineers went to get the file, it could not be found. So were they a gift from an anonymous Italian Sculptor or commissioned by Disneyland? We may never know, but like all things Disney, it makes for a great story.
(EN: 204 / 205 / 206 / 286 / 287)

48

ABOVE: The full scene of the statues with the fish above water blowing water. Notice how even in a picture, that Snow White still appears to be taller than the dwarfs. This is due to her placement above the dwarfs and slightly behind which makes her appear to be much farther away and thus make her appear to be the correct height.

RIGHT: The fish in the pond at the base of the waterfall circle as they blow water streams. If they are not there when you go to see the statues, don't worry. They periodically submerge, but give them a couple of minutes and they will come up and begin to dance again.

Disney decided to duplicate the statues for display at Disneyland Paris, but made the same mistake with the size of Snow White. They had to use a similar solution to the one at Disneyland. When they built a set for Disneyland Tokyo, they corrected the size issue. When the statues arrived in Japan, they were sent back as they wanted an exact copy of the scene in Disneyland. (EN: 207 / 296)

AUTHOR'S NOTE: Again as I mentioned on the page about the 'wooden indian', this is another example of an original being replaced with an exact duplicate. More examples will be discussed in the chapter WOW, *That's Interesting!*.

ABOVE: Close up of Snow White. Notice the beautiful details.

BELOW Close up of Sneezy and Dopey. These are just wonderful statues with so much character.

BELOW ALL: **UL**-One of the most interesting Urban Legends is that Rolly Crump was inspired by Leota Toombs' home-made jewelry for the design of the spires and other gold colored parts of the it's a small world facade. **FALSE**: I contacted Rolly Crump about this and he told me that he had never heard this story before, and that it was completely false. The only person who inspired his design for the facade was the wonderful Imagineer Mary Blair. Mary was the original stylist for it's a small world, and was a great friend and inspiration to Rolly. (EN: 49 / 50 / 51)

BELOW: Imagine the spires hanging upside-down. It's easy to imagine them as earrings.

AUTHOR'S NOTE: You may have noticed the spelling of it's a small world is lower case and thought it was a mistake. That is actually the proper way to spell it. Just look at the marquee in the top picture.

UL-Disneyland was issued its own ZIP code by the US Postal Service. **FALSE**: When walking around Disneyland, you will see many mail boxes around the Park. This has most likely helped to create the legend that Disneyland has its own ZIP code. However, they are functional mail boxes that you can use to mail anything from Disneyland post cards to your personal mail (as I have done on many trips). The mail boxes are maintained and serviced by Disneyland Cast Members (DL). Each day, the Cast Members empty the boxes and send the mail to the Disney administration office. They in turn transport the mail to the local post office with their daily mail. (EN: 268)

ABOVE: As you can see from this label, the mail boxes are maintained by Disneyland Cast Members.

LEFT: This is one of the first mail boxes you encounter once you enter Disneyland. It can be found on the left side of the right tunnel. I have used this mail box many times.

LEFT: Once on Main Street, U.S.A., you can find mail boxes attached to the gas lamp posts.

RIGHT: Ever wanted to send mail to a ghost? This mail box is located just inside the gates of Haunted Mansion. Unfortunately, you can't leave your ghost mail here, as this is not an actual mail box. It holds a phone for cast members working the gate.

BELOW LEFT: Ever wonder how you will mail things in the future? This mail box is located on the left side of Innoventions in Tomorrowland, just before you get to the restrooms. Well, mail may be all electronic in the future, but for now, you can keep using this one.

RIGHT: This well worn mail box can be found on the front of the Briar Patch hat store in Critter Country.

BELOW LEFT: After mailing a letter in the future, you can also mail a letter in the past. This mail box is located in front of Silver Spur Supplies in Frontierland.

BELOW RIGHT: This mail box is located at the Golden Horseshoe Revue. It is on the right side of the building, just before you get to the Stage Door Cafe.

LEFT: As we've seen, not every mail box is real. This one, located in front of Goofy's House, has several fun items in it, but don't leave your letters.

BELOW: The full sized mail box located in front of the Toontown Post Office isn't real either. Go ahead and pull the handle for some fun.

BELOW LEFT: These mail boxes can be found inside the Toontown Post Office. Twist their knobs for more fun.

ABOVE: **UL**-The cave entrance on the back side of Big Thunder Mountain is the original entrance to Rainbow Caverns. **FALSE**: Although looking at maps overlaid with aerial photographs appear to show it in the correct location, the current rock work is clearly not original when you look at photographs of the old entrance. I also had the opportunity to ask a former Imagineer about this, and he confirmed that it is not one of the left-over parts of the former attraction. Check out the chapter "Gone but Still There" to see a couple of tunnel entrances that did remain. (EN: 32)

LEFT: **UL**-The smoking jacket hanging in the Lilly Belle is the one Walt Disney used to wear. **TRUE and FALSE**: The original jacket was the one that Walt had worn. However, wanting to preserve it from damage over time, the jacket was removed and replaced with an exact duplicate. (EN:30)

BELOW: If you ever get the chance to ride in the Lilly Belle, you get a wonderful souvenir ticket to commemorate your experience.

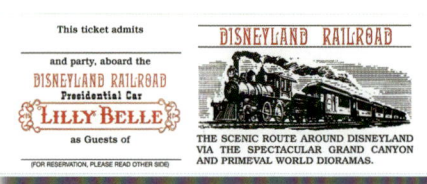

UL-The 5 ton petrified redwood tree in Frontierland was given to Lillian Disney by Walt Disney for their 31st wedding anniversary. **FALSE**: This story has a very long history and was apparently started by Walt himself. The tree was actually found and bought on their anniversary trip. It was actually purchased as part of the Frontierland expansion, which included Mineral Hall. In addition to purchasing this tree, Walt also purchased one ton of petrified tree debris. You will note that the plaque does say donated by "Mrs. Walt Disney" but does not tell the famous story.
(EN:79)

UL-Whenever Walt Disney was in the Park or staying in his apartment, they would turn on a light in the window to let Cast members know he was in residence. **FALSE:** This is a wonderful story still told by Cast Members today. I was fortunate enough to have a friend contact two of Walt Disney's family members, and neither remembers this happening. (EN: 140)

Even from a practical point of view, this wouldn't make sense. First of all, the light would not be visible during the day. At night, it would light up the apartment, making it inconvenient for anyone sleeping there. In addition, there are famous stories, such as the one where Walt showed up in his robe late one night when construction workers were doing some maintenance on the Park. Walt reportedly surprised them and offered to take them to the Citrus Bar as he had the key. Cast Members clearly would not have been surprised if this system were in place. The light is a loving tribute to Walt Disney and I am glad that they are doing it.

ABOVE: The light shines in the window as a reminder that Walt is always watching over the Park.

RIGHT: During the holiday season, the lamp is replaced with a lighted Christmas tree.

58

Disneyland Pays Tributes

Many people have contributed to the success of Disneyland. Most people are aware that the Windows on Main Street, U.S.A., and other locations, which pay tribute to some of these people. But, are you aware that there are many other tributes to people hidden in plain site around the Park? In addition, there are tributes to past attractions, movies, locations, and much more.

ABOVE: One of the first tributes I became aware of was this air lock in the Space Mountain queue (DL). It can be found as you are walking down the last tunnel before entering the launch bay. If you look up about two thirds of the way down this tunnel, you will see this hatch on the ceiling. It pays tribute to John Hench, one of the truly great Imagineers. Hench was one of the original Imagineers who worked on many Disney attractions and was a key player in the construction of Walt Disney World. He was also a color expert, making colors work with each other, and adding to the Guests' experiences. One of my favorite anecdotes was when he was once told to just, "paint it white." To which he replied, and I paraphrase, "Which one? I see 34 shades of white." (EN:137)

BELOW: In the queue for Buzz Lightyear Astro Blasters, Buzz Lightyear is briefing us on our mission to save the universe by preventing Emperor Zurg from getting all of the batteries. Several batteries can be seen in the queue. They look pretty ordinary, but look at the "Made In" label. It says the batteries were made in Glendale, California. This is the home of Walt Disney Imagineering (WDI), the part of The Walt Disney Company responsible for coming up with all of the wonderful attractions, and most of the details, we love so much. (EN: 295)

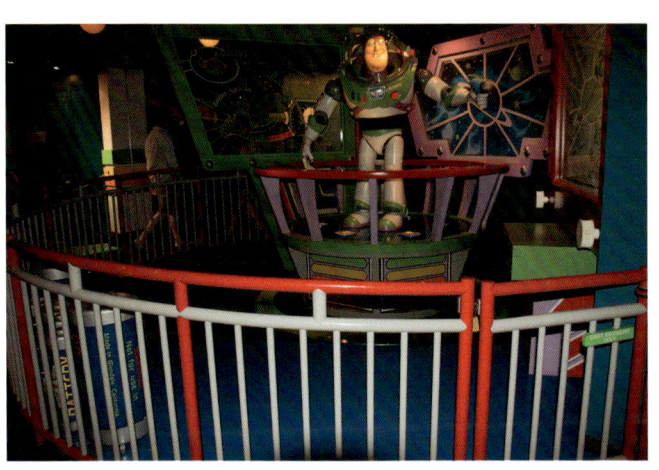

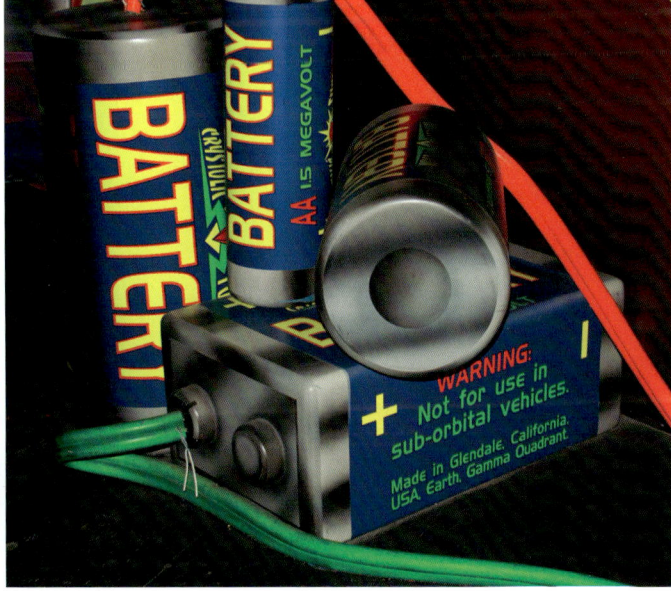

ABOVE: A more subtle tribute can be found over at Star Tours - The Adventure Continues. When you first enter the queue, look up and to the rear of the Star Speeder 1000. You will see that its number is 1401. The flight is also called 1401 during the attraction when flight control is talking with C3PO. What is the significance of 1401? Walt Disney Imagineering is located at 1401 Flower Street in Glendale. (EN: 162)

BELOW: Next time you are in Toontown, take a look at the hills above Minnie Mouse's House. You will see some faux trees that form the letters WDI. This is a tribute to Walt Disney Imagineering, the part of The Walt Disney Company responsible for designing the Disney theme parks, attractions, stores, restaurants, hotels, and so much more. They are also responsible for all the wonderful details you see in my Seen Un-Seen books. (EN: 136)

ABOVE: As you travel through Roger Rabbit's Car Toon Spin, if you're looking in the correct direction, you will see two Jack-In-The-Boxes that just popped out. One has a J on its box and the other has an M. These are tributes to two of the Imagineers who worked on the attraction. These caricatures are tributes to Joe Lanzisero and Marcelo (Moe) Vignali. Mr. Vignali actually drew the caricatures himself. The Jack-In-The-Boxes are known as Moe and Joe. (EN: 211 / 212 / 213)

ABOVE AND LEFT: Just as you are about to exit it's a small world, look to your left. There is a postage stamp shaped picture with the classic kids of the world boat. Or is it? Look again and you will see that one of the children has curly hair and a squiggly mouth. Is that Charlie Brown? (EN: 310)

BELOW LEFT AND RIGHT: During the design phase of it's a small world for the 1964-1965 New York World's Fair, Rolly Crump was assigned the task of designing The Tower of the Four Winds. Since Walt Disney wanted a weenie (DL) for the front of the attraction. Rolly had a hobby earlier in his career of building mobiles and propellers. Walt apparently remembered Rolly's work, so he asked him to include them in the Tower's design. Rolly designed a very elegant tower, but due to construction concerns by the engineers, the tower was built much more "bulky" than Rolly envisioned. Rolly never quite liked the final version and when it came time to bring it's a small world back to Disneyland, the tower was cut up and reportedly dumped into the ocean. However, if you look at the marquee at the entrance of it's a small world, you will notice it's overall shape has the distinctive look of the Tower of the Four Winds. This is a tribute to the now iconic Tower of the Four Winds. (EN:52 / 53)

RIGHT: Like much of Disneyland, this tower gets a holiday overlay.

Mary Blair is a well-known Imagineer who started at the Walt Disney Studios in 1939. She worked on such Disney classics as *Cinderella, Alice in Wonderland, Peter Pan, The Three Caballeros,* and *Saludos Amigos.* She was one of the studio artists who went with Walt Disney on his Good Neighbor Program tour to Latin America in 1941. This trip really helped to make Mary Blair's style so unique. When work on the 1964-1965 New York World's Fair started, Mary Blair was asked to contribute to it's a small world attraction. Rolly Crump was asked to work with her. He eagerly agreed as he loved Mary's style. Mary Blair was the stylist for the attraction and as such, was responsible for the final look. Rolly decided there should be a tribute to Mary so when the attraction was built in New York, he added a blonde haired doll with very stylized clothing.

ABOVE: In the France section, there is a representation of the Eiffel Tower.

LEFT AND BELOW: About one-third of the way up is a doll flying a ribbon and balloon. The style of clothes is clearly not like the others in the scene. The doll is a wonderful tribute to Mary Blair. (EN: 45 / 46 / 47 / 48 / 56 / 299 / 300)

65

LEFT AND BELOW: On opening day, the Carnation Café was the Carnation Ice Cream Parlor. As part of the Streetmosphere (DL), Walt Disney had Bob Gurr design a classic looking ice cream truck. Carnation built the truck, and it was there for many years. (EN: 311)

During its heyday, it was a popular photo opp. When the ice cream parlor closed in 1997, a tribute to the truck was added to the sign of the new Carnation Café.

You can still see the truck today at Camp Korey at Carnation Farm, Carnation, WA (near Seattle). (EN: 312)

RIGHT: As you enter the Jolly Holiday Bakery, look left, and you will see this mural. Prior to becoming the Jolly Holiday Bakery, it was many different stores, including an Annual Passholder (AP) center and the Plaza Pavilion Restaurant. This restaurant had a wonderful mural depicting a tree with all sorts of food from the United States and Europe. Unfortunately, the mural was destroyed during the renovation, reportedly due to health concerns about the wall it was painted on. As a tribute to this lost piece of art, a new mural was created to honor the original. (EN: 135)

LEFT AND BELOW: In the Hub is one of the most iconic statues of the Park, entitled "Partners". Sculpted by Blaine Gibson, it is a wonderful tribute to Walt Disney's and Mickey Mouse's partnership. Rarely does a Disney Imagineer get direct credit for their work. It is always considered a team effort. But if you walk around to the back and look at the right side of the base, you will see Blaine Gibson was allowed to sign his work. A very rare tribute.

ABOVE: One of the most popular Disneyland attractions is Big Thunder Mountain Railroad. In fact, it is so popular, it has been replicated at three other Parks. While standing in the queue, you will see two direction signs. Look closely at the one farthest away. You will notice that, except for Rainbow Ridge (the location of Thunder Mountain), the sign is pointing to locations thousands of miles (or kilometers) away. This sign is actually pointing out the direction and distance to each of its sister attractions: Walt Disney World (Tumbleweed 2496 miles), Disneyland Paris (Thunder Mesa 9258 km (5740 miles)), and Disneyland Hong Kong (Grizzly Gulch 11743 km (7281 miles)). (EN: 54)

ABOVE AND BELOW: This tribute not only pays homage to a movie, but shows the wonderful humor that Imagineers often use. This tribute is for the movie *Indiana Jones and the Last Crusade*. In the movie, the elder Dr. Jones (played by Sean Connery) has an argument where he is chastising the younger Dr. Jones (played by Harrison Ford) for using the name Indiana. The elder Dr. Jones famously says, "We named the dog Indiana."

This tribute can only be seen from the Disneyland Railroad. While riding the segment between the New Orleans Frontierland station and Toontown station, you pass behind Big Thunder Ranch. You will see a small building on the right side of the train with a bunch of supplies. In front of the building is a dog house with the name Indiana painted on it. (EN: 290)

Side note: This is also one of the three locations where vehicles can actually cross over the train tracks mentioned in the Disneyland Railroad chapter. In the picture above, you can see the gate that leads to Big Thunder Ranch.

THIS PAGE: The man who was literally responsible for the construction of Disneyland was Admiral Joe Fowler. He held degrees from the Naval Academy and MIT, and was,

by trade, a naval architect. During World War II, Admiral Fowler ran the naval shipyards in San Francisco. He knew large project organization, man power use, budgeting, and time management. He was well known for his "Can Do!" attitude, so he was the perfect person to run the construction of Disneyland. He often insisted on using the best building practices of the time, which are still paying off today. He built Disneyland to last. While building the Rivers of America, Joe insisted on building a dry dock to be used for maintenance on the Mark Twain. Everyone thought it was a waste and called it "Joe's Hole". After the first time it proved useful, it was then called Fowler's Harbor.

(EN:112) After Disneyland's opening, he was in charge of operations and supervised most of the major Plussing (DL) of the Park, including the Matterhorn, Submarine Voyage, Monorail, Haunted Mansion, and Pirates of the Caribbean. Later, Admiral Fowler would manage the construction of Walt Disney World. (EN: 55)

Ray Bradbury was a great friend to Walt Disney. Ray referred to it as a "quiet friendship". Walt would talk to Ray about many of his ideas and Ray provided input for Disneyland, the 1964-1965 New York World's Fair, and even EPCOT. After Walt's death, Ray helped get a lot of Walt's original ideas into EPCOT, and even wrote the original script for Spaceship Earth.

In 1972, Ray published a fantasy novel called The Halloween Tree. (EN: 214)

ABOVE: This tree in front of the Silver Spur Supplies in Frontierland is converted to "The Halloween Tree" each Halloween. (EN: 114)

BELOW: At night.

ABOVE: This dedication plaque is placed by the tree to explain its origins. The illustrations in the four corners were created by Joe Luganni and were originally used in the book. (EN: 111 / 113)

70

ABOVE: While walking through the Jungle Cruise queue, there are many wonderful artifacts to look at and keep you entertained. The "blue prints" for the Congo Queen boat hangs on the wall just after the dispatcher's office. To most, it just looks like an interesting paper hung on the wall, but if you look in the lower right hand corner, you will see that the drawing was checked by H. Goff. There is also a minor tribute to WED (DL). Harper Goff was one of the primary designers of Disneyland. Goff was hired by Walt Disney after a chance meeting in England. He was initially hired to help with Walt's recent entry into making live action films. One of Goff's first projects was to story board (DL) *20,000 Leagues Under the Sea*. He was supposed to base the story boards on a True Life Adventure nature film, but instead based his work on Jules Vernes' original story. Walt was initially upset, but was won over by Goff's great work. The distinctive design of the Nautilus is some of his best known work. When Disneyland entered its design phase, he did much of the work for Main Street, U.S.A. and Adventureland. He is best know for all his work on Jungle Cruise. Goff can also be heard as the banjo player for the Fire House Five Plus 2. (EN: 88)

RIGHT: Close up of the tribute for Harper Goff from the picture above.

One of the most popular attractions that no longer exists at Disneyland is the Country Bear Jamboree. If you walk around Critter Country, you can find many tributes to this wonderful former attraction.

BELOW: As you enter Critter Country, you will see a restaurant on your right called the Hungry Bear Restaurant.

BELOW: If you go up to the counter, you will see a sign behind the Cast Members featuring The Five Bear Rugs with various food items replacing their instruments. Clockwise: Fred (plays the mouth harp or harmonica), Ted (plays the corn jug and wash board), Zeb (plays the fiddle), Zeke (plays the banjo and taps his foot on a dishpan, and is also considered the leader of the band), and Tennessee (plays the "thing" which only has one string). (EN: 116 / 117 / 118)

BELOW LEFT: As you walk to the back of Critter Country, you will find Pooh Corner. They have all sorts of great gifts, but the best part is the candy section where they actually make various candy delights. Go up to the window and watch them make these treats, but don't forget to look at the pictures behind the Cast Members. There you will see a picture of Winnie the Pooh with Gomer. (EN: 115)

BELOW RIGHT: And a picture of Winnie the Pooh with Teddi Barra.

BELOW: If you go outside and look up at the left side of Pooh's Corner, you will see another tribute. This one says Teddi Barra's Swingin' Arcade, which pays tribute to both Teddi Barra and the arcade that use to be housed in this store.

ABOVE: There are many wonderful horses on the King Arthur Carrousel. The horse with all the bells is known as Jingles. It pays tribute to one of Disney's most beloved movies, *Mary Poppins* and the actress who portrayed her, Julie Andrews.

BELOW LEFT: The saddle has a pair of Mary's boots, the initials JA (Julie Andrews), a silhouette of Mary Poppins, and a "50" for the 50th anniversary of the movie.

BELOW RIGHT: The blanket has Mary's umbrella. It also has a Hidden Mickey.

OK, A Few More Hidden Mickeys

LETTERS

U.S. MAIL

Hidden Mickeys are as popular as ever. This book is still not a Hidden Mickey guide book, but I have to show a few of my favorites.

LEFT: As a photographer, how could I not use this one first? This camera can be found on a shelf above the photo viewing stations in the Main Street Photo Supply Company. Take a close look at the lens.

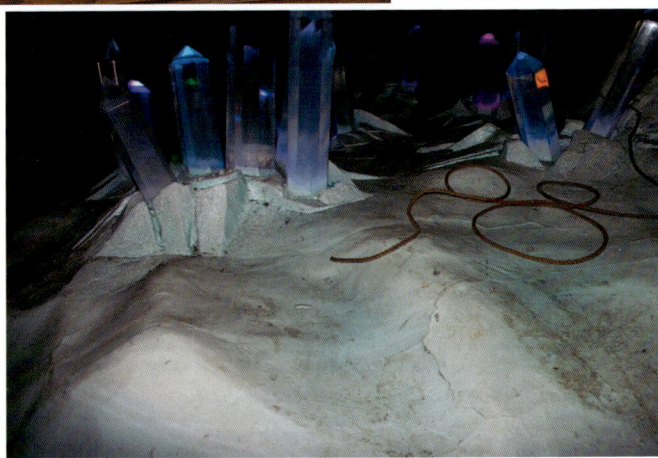

RIGHT: Another one of my favorites can be found in the Ice Cave on top of the Matterhorn. Who ever coiled this rope wasn't too careful. Or were they?

LEFT: Next time you enter the scanner room in the Star Tours' queue, look to your right to see the REX droids. Just past their crates, you will see a little droid sitting on top of a crate. Check out the shadow behind him.

AUTHOR'S NOTE: There is lively discussion on when the Imagineers and Disney Artists began putting Hidden Mickeys into attractions and pictures. Some of them may have just been created by accident, and once noticed, were adopted over time as a Hidden Mickey. In addition, anytime someone sees 3 spheres together, they may think it is a Hidden Mickey. Some are, and some are not. But if you see one, and it brings you joy, that is what finding Hidden Mickeys is all about. Just enjoy them. The ones I have included in this book are generally accepted as Hidden Mickeys today, even if they were not originally intended to be a Hidden Mickey.

LEFT: This statue of Mr. Toad can be found in the queue of Mr. Toad's Wild Ride. Just after you enter the building, you turn to your left and this statue is standing in the window. Hundreds of people pass this statue each day. How many take the time to look him in the eyes? If you do, you will notice two small, red Hidden Mickeys in his eye. (EN: 90)

QUIZ: In Disney language, all rides are referred to as Attractions. However, the proper name for this attraction is Mr. Toad's Wild Ride. How many attractions actually have "ride" in their name and can you name them? (Answer EN: 39)

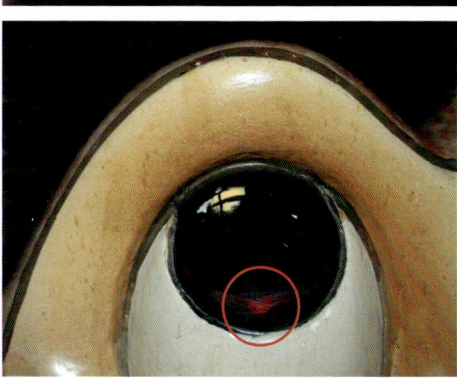

ABOVE: This close up of Mr. Toad's right eye has the Hidden Mickey highlighted with a red circle.

RIGHT: This is a close-up of Mr. Toad's left eye, again with the Hidden Mickey circled.

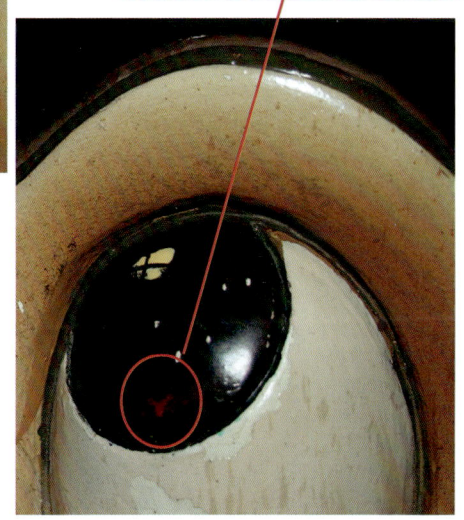

RIGHT: One of the more obvious, but still often over looked, Hidden Mickeys is the Fruit Cart on Center Street off of Main Street, U.S.A.. The Imagineers have created a wonderful Hidden Mickey on the axle of the cart. (EN: 319)

LEFT: Close up of the Hidden Mickey.

ABOVE AND RIGHT: Another one of my favorite Hidden Mickeys can be found here. If you are thinking this is just a pile of horse shoes, you'd be wrong. The bulk of the pile is actually old mule shoes. That's right, this is a left over pile of shoes used by the mules from the Rainbow Ridge Mule Pack / Pack Mules Through Nature's Wonderland. When the area was re-furbished into the Big Thunder Ranch area, the shoes were left and a Hidden Tribute to Mickey placed in the pile. By some accounts, this Hidden Mickey was rearranged after the 2006 acquisition of Oswald the Lucky

Rabbit back into the Disney family to be a "Hidden Oswald". It's officially listed as a hidden Mickey. Which ever you see, this is a fun one to find. (EN: 241 / 267 / 314)

ABOVE AND RIGHT: Next time you are in the Briar Patch in Critter Country, look on the shelf above the cash register.

LEFT AND BELOW (2): Have you wondered how long the Imagineers have been including Hidden Mickeys in the Parks? The Mark Twain was an opening day attraction. Look at the ornamental iron works between the 2 smoke stacks. If you look about half way between the center star and the stacks, you will see a Hidden Mickey. (EN: 91 /92 / 316)

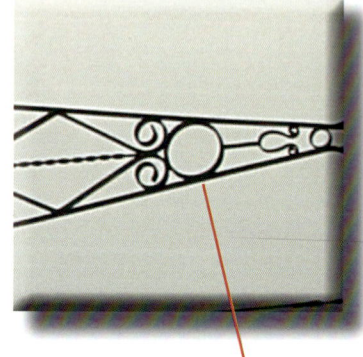

BELOW AND RIGHT (2): On the right side of the Mark Twain / Columbia loading dock is a snack store. If you go around to the right side of it, you will see this mural. It includes the same Hidden Mickey and a little bonus. Look closely at the deck just before the bow, and you will see a real Hidden Mickey in the crowd. (EN: 93)

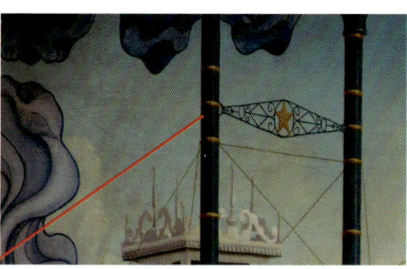

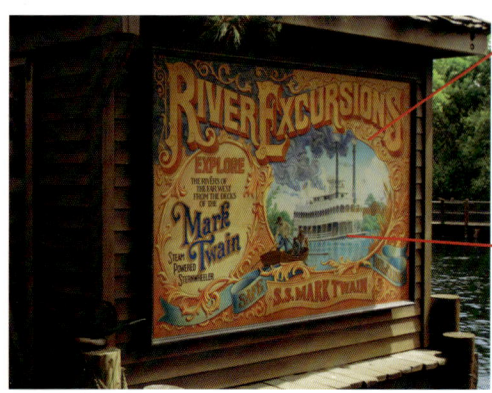

ABOVE: After you launch from the docks in Pirates of the Caribbean, you float through the bayou. There are many interesting things to see, including lily pads. But have you looked closely at these? They are located on the right side just before you pass the Blue Bayou restaurant. (EN: 317)

BELOW: After going down the two water falls, you enter the grotto. The first scene on the right is a beach where a sword fight over pirate booty has taken place. The treasure chest is now empty, taken by the victor. Or is it? Look again, and you might see some abalone shells in a familiar shape. Not all Hidden Mickeys are official Walt Disney Imagineering (WDI) ones. This one, and many others, are done by Cast Members. They often come and go as WDI does maintenance on an attraction and removes unofficial Hidden Mickeys.

LEFT: The holidays at Disneyland bring many extra visual treats for Guests. The Haunted Mansion gets its Nightmare Before Christmas (NBC) overlay, known as Haunted Mansion Holiday. Look closely and you may see a few Hidden Mickeys to help celebrate. This one can be found in the Ballroom scene.

BELOW: To the left of the entrance to the Haunted Mansion is a Fast Pass Distribution garden. It is only open during busy times of the year. To the left of the entrance is this potted plant. Take a closer look at the handles and main body. They should form a familiar shape by now.

BELOW AND BELOW LEFT: You can even find a Hidden Mickey on some mail boxes. This one can be found on the mail box outside the Heraldry Shoppe in Fantasyland.

BELOW RIGHT: Did you also notice the skull on the mail box? I learned about this one from a video on the internet. (EN: 44) My research could not find a definitive answer about why this is present. Some people speculate that it could be related to the Heraldry Shoppe it sits in front of. Others think that it is because the Disney Villains, and later Villains Lair, were in the same location. I think that, because it is in Fantasyland, is located next door to Perter Pan's Flight, and there are other tributes that are related to Peter Pan, it is probably a tribute to Skull Rock. Skull Rock is part of the Disneyland Peter Pan story and was a rock formation that was part of a cove that surrounded the extinct Chicken of the Sea Restaurant (Chicken of the Sea Pirate Ship and Restaurant / Captain Hook's Galley) that was removed during the 1982 renovation. (EN: 57 / 89)

QUIZ: Can you names all the stores that were housed in this location?
(Answer EN: 59)

ABOVE AND RIGHT: Monstro makes a wonderful entrance to the Storybook Land Canal Boats. If you look above the right side of his mouth, you will see a Hidden Mickey.

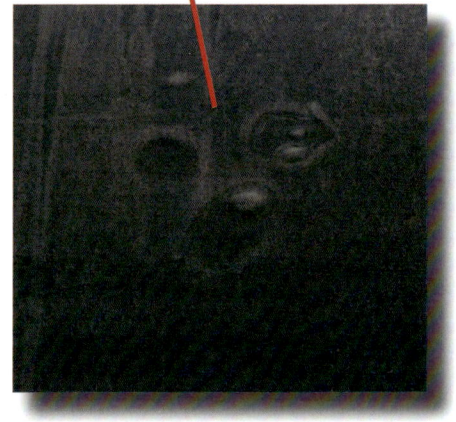

BELOW AND BELOW RIGHT: In Buzz Lightyear Astro Blasters, you will find Buzz giving a briefing to the new cadets. Just after you enter this area you will see a galaxy map and monitors. On the Sector 2 monitor, look at the green spheres that make up the planet. There is a classic Hidden Mickey.

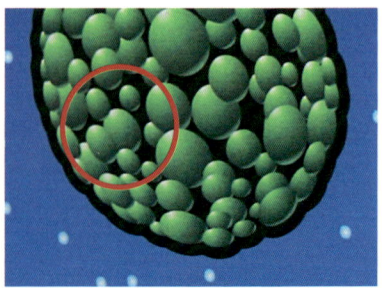

RIGHT: Another Dark Ride (DL) in Fantasyland that gets in on the Hidden Mickey fun is Pinocchio's Daring Journey. As your travel through the attraction, you will come to the Pleasure Island scene. This is where all the bad boys are turned into donkeys. In that scene, you will see a large popcorn box that is over flowing. Three kernels have fallen out and form a Hidden Mickey. (EN: 94)

LEFT AND BELOW: As you walk through the tunnel from the Princess Fantasy Faire to Rancho del Zocalo Restaurante, stop at the entrance to the Fairy Tale Treasures Shop. Look up at the wooden rafters. You have to be to one side in order to see past the lower beam. Look where they meet. It's hard to see, but look closely. (EN: 95)

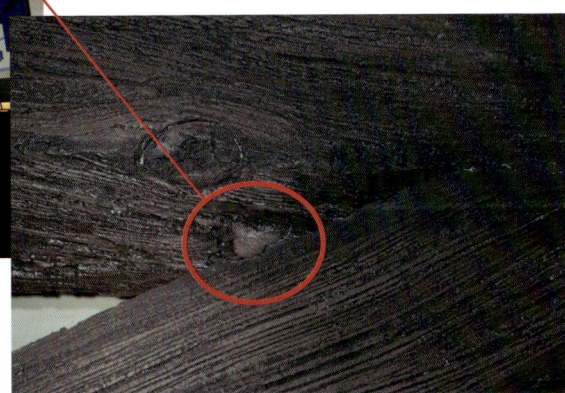

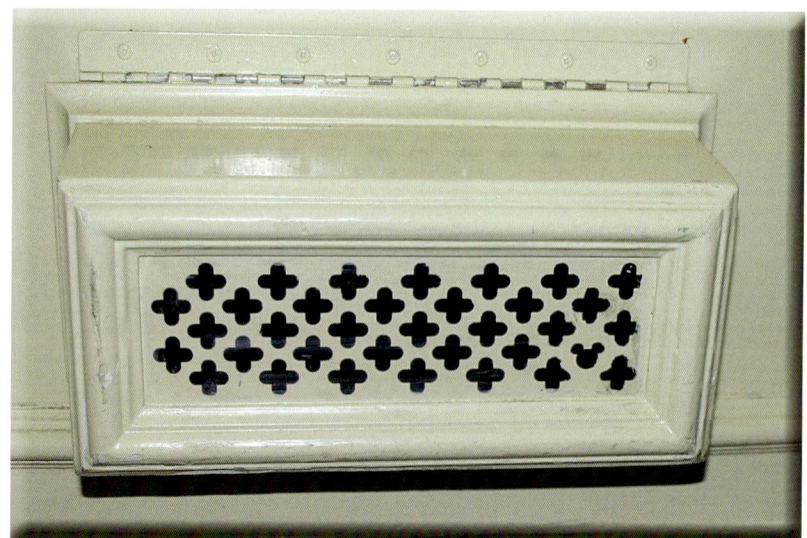

ABOVE AND LEFT: The next time you go to the Golden Horseshoe to enjoy a show or a snack, take a look at the base of the stage. You will notice in the center a vent like many others in the attraction. Only this one has a hole that is very familiar.

BELOW: I will end this chapter like I ended it in my first book, Seen, Un-Seen Disneyland, with another Hidden Alternative. On Pirates of the Caribbean, after you pass the captain's quarters, but before you get to the pirates booty (Treasure Room), this familiar looking rock formation can be seen. Could this be a Hidden Pluto or Zero?

I Think I've Seen That Before?

As you look into the Disneyland Fire Station on Main Street, you will see an old horse drawn fire engine. When you walk around Frontierland, you may have seen surreys or even a stage coach displayed around the land. They come and go, are moved from location to location, and are re-decorated from time to time. Disneyland really did a nice job collecting these coaches to Plus (DL) the Park. Actually, the fire engine and coaches have been around Disneyland for a lot longer than people realize. Many were part of the opening day attractions on Main Street or Frontierland.

ABOVE: The horse drawn fire engine at the Disneyland Fire Station #105 (next to City Hall) looks like a wonderful detail that the Imagineers added to create a great photo opportunity. However, on the opening day of Disneyland, the fire engine was actually an attraction you could ride up and down Main Street. Walk around to the rear of the fire engine and you will see that there is a step to go up into the area where the fire hose would normally be kept. The fire hose bed has been converted into seating on each side with plenty of leg room. Of the three styles of Main Street vehicles that operated on opening day, the fire engines lasted the shortest at only 5 years. It was then retired to its present location in the Main Street Fire station. The Surreys remained until 1971, while the Horse-Drawn Streetcars are still in use today. (EN: 141)

The fire engine is on permanent static display in the Disneyland Fire Station. However, the following 5 pages show various coaches that are moved around the Park, or even sometimes taken back stage.

You will often see many different Surreys and even a stage coach in Frontierland. The stage coach was part of the Disneyland Stage Line, later renamed the Rainbow Mountain Stage Coach line, that ran through Nature's Wonderland along with the Mine Trains, Mules and the Conestoga Wagons. The stage coaches remained in operation until 1959, when they were retired. One of the stage coaches was pulled out of retirement in 1980 for Disneyland's 25th anniversary. It was pulled out again in 2005 to celebrate the 50th anniversary of Disneyland. You can still see this stage coach being used around Frontierland for streetmosphere (DL). (EN: 142 / 151 / 240)

ABOVE: The stage coach positioned just outside the entrance to the Big Thunder Ranch.

LEFT: Inside Big Thunder Ranch Jamboree area. The stage coach is decorated for the 4th of July celebrations.

In addition to the side loading surreys used on Main Street, Disneyland also used rear loading surreys. These surreys loaded in much the same way as the horse drawn fire engine was loaded. They are not often mentioned in my research sources, but historical pictures from Disneyland-related web pages show them in use. I was not able to get a definitive date on when they stopped operations, but it is most likely in 1971 when the other Main Street surreys stopped operations. (EN: 144 / 149)

ABOVE: Big Thunder Ranch Barbecue area dressed up for Spring.

BELOW: Big Thunder Ranch Barbecue area dressed up for Christmas.

ABOVE: This rear loading surreys shown on display at the entrance to Big Thunder Ranch.

LEFT: The same surrey displayed at the entrance to Big Thunder Ranch Barbecue. This time it is dressed up to celebrate Spring.

RIGHT: In this picture, the surrey is displayed in front of Miss Chris' cabin, inside Big Thunder Ranch. It is dressed up for Christmas. During this time of year, Miss Chris' cabin is used as a meet and greet with Santa Claus.

There are also several smaller coaches used around Frontierland. Probably due to their size and their accessibility, they do not appear to have been used as an attraction, but some are similar to ones used in parades. Never the less, they add to the wonderful details of Frontierland. (EN: 280)

LEFT: This little surrey is shown in the Big Thunder Ranch Jamboree. It is being used as part of the Springtime Roundup celebration.

RIGHT: This surrey resembles a classic Model T automobile and is shown in Big Thunder Ranch Barbecue. It is decorated to celebrate the 4th of July.

LEFT: The same surrey as above in Big Thunder Ranch Barbecue, only this time it is decorated to celebrate Christmas.

LEFT: This surrey is shown displayed along the Big Thunder Trail, between Big Thunder Ranch Barbecue and Fantasyland. It is decorated for Halloween.

RIGHT: The same surrey displayed in front of Big Thunder Ranch.

LEFT: The same surrey in front of Big Thunder Ranch, this time decorated for the 4th of July celebrations.

On January 9th, 1987, Star Tours had its grand opening at Disneyland, and the Park remained open for 60 hours to celebrate. The captain of your Star Speeder 3000 was a droid recently put into service, though still slightly buggy. He was an RX-24 droid, but was commonly referred to as REX. Captain REX took you on the same adventure each time, ultimately resulting in the destruction of the Death Star.

On July 27, 2010, the last original tours ran, and on June 3, 2011 a new prequel version began operations. The new attraction was called Star Tours: The Adventures Continue. As a tribute to the original attraction, and to help with the story that REX was in the future, one of the original REX droids can now be seen in the queue. Just after you pass C-3PO and enter the customs security area, look to your right. (EN: 146 / 147 / 148 / 150)

ABOVE: One of the original REX droids that flew the Star Speeder 3000's in the original attraction. Note he has a defective tag on him, indicating he had problems from the start.

RIGHT: These RX series droids are slightly different from the RX-24 droids and have a different color scheme. They do not have defective tags on them. The current attraction flies the Star Speeder 1000 series and a mobile droid for a pilot. These are possibly the droids to be used on other Star Speeders such as the 2000's. The lack of legs could be due to costs. Why does the pilot need to leave the ship? For that matter, why isn't he just an integrated computer? But where is the fun in that?

Quiz time: This is an easy one. Do you know who voiced Rex in the original Star Tours?
(EN: 145 Answer)

One of the more famous extinct attractions is the Mine Train Through Nature's Wonderland. This attraction occupied the space that is now home to Big Thunder Mountain Railroad, Big Thunder Ranch, and more. This wonderful attraction was home to over 200 animals, and shared its space with the stage coaches (1955 - 1960), conestoga wagons (1955-1959), and pack mule (1955 - 1973) attractions. Sadly, in 1977, Mine Train was closed. As with so many former attractions, and as a cost savings measure, many of the props and animals were re-purposed into the Big Thunder Mountain attractions in both Disneyland and Magic Kingdom. (EN: 68 / 187 / 191 / 192 / 193 /194)

ABOVE: One of the more famous residents that was rumored to have made the move to Big Thunder Mountain is the dynamite eating goat. He has been seen wearing several different coats, but is always chewing on that dynamite. Although a very interesting character to look at over time, he was not a part of Mine Train Through Nature's Wonderland. Here he can be seen in his newly re-furbished 2014 coat.

RIGHT: The goat wearing his 2012 coat.

BELOW: The goat is in is 2007 coat.

ABOVE: The coyotes can be seen just before entering the tunnel leading to the second lift.

BELOW AND RIGHT: The vulture, on their high perches, can be seen from many parts of the attraction, including the loading area.

ABOVE AND BELOW RIGHT: The rattlesnakes and the tortoises are on the left side of the second lift. Careful that those rattlers don't strike you as you go by.

BELOW INSET: This guy looks like he is getting ready to ride the tracks.

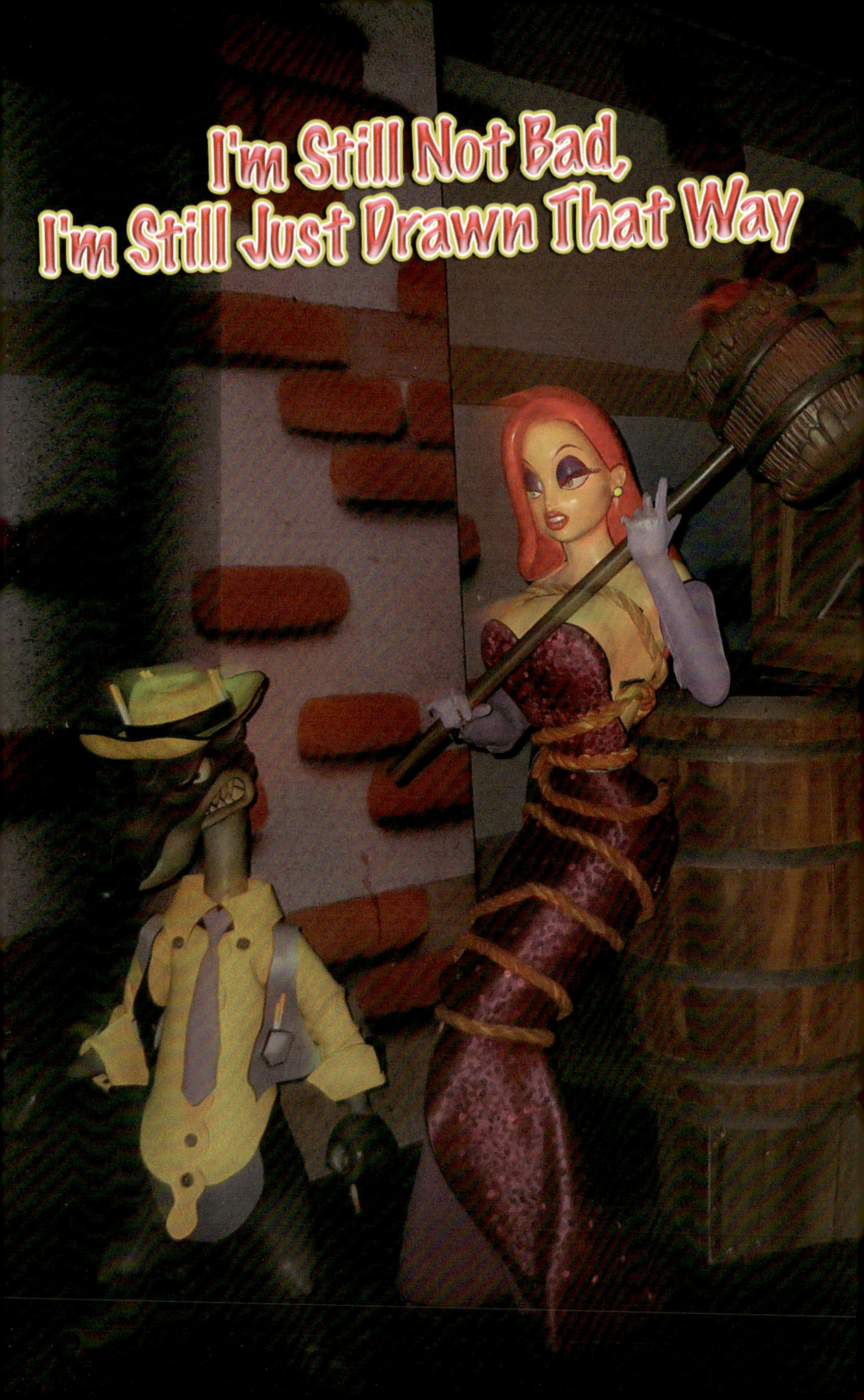
I'm Still Not Bad,
I'm Still Just Drawn That Way

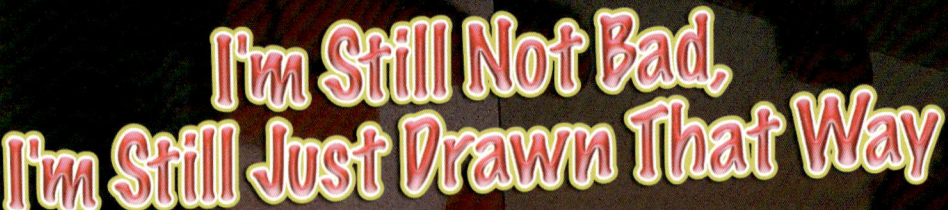

Disney has a long tradition of being very clean, wholesome, family oriented, and kid friendly. But, that doesn't stop them from stepping out occasionally in a tasteful and humorous way.

Let's start this chapter with my favorite "just drawn that way" character, Jessica Rabbit, from the movie *Who Framed Roger Rabbit*. Jessica is the one who coined that now famous phrase, so it seems fitting.

ABOVE: A scene from Roger Rabbit's Car Toon Spin. Here, the weasels have captured Jessica, tied her up, and are trying to put her into the trunk of their car. Do they have a big surprise coming, or what?

LEFT: In the Roger Rabbit's Car Toon Spin queue, you see Baby Herman's room. You may recognize the pin-up calendar from Seen, Un-Seen Disneyland. Look carefully at the wall paper and you will see Jessica Rabbit's silhouette.

RIGHT: A blown up and darkened look at the wall paper.

ABOVE: This sign can be seen on both sides of The Golden Horseshoe. By today's standards, it's pretty tame. But, for the time period it was pretty wild. Let's take a closer look.

BELOW: The first thing you notice is all of the leg the can-can dancers are showing off. The Golden Horseshoe Revue was also famous for its can-can dancers.

LEFT AND RIGHT: These dancers can always be counted on for high kickin' and sassy fun.

Look at the ornate drawing below and above each figure. Did you notice the hidden Mickeys? (EN: 318)

ABOVE: The signs explain, in detail, what you can expect to see in the show.

RIGHT: But wait! What does that say on the bottom left of the sign? No, it's not what it sounds like at first. This is just another term for the "Fairer Sex" or females.

ABOVE: Once inside, mosey on up to the bar to get your favorite drinks, food, and snacks. Now look up at the mirror behind the bartenders. You will see this beauty.

ABOVE AND RIGHT: Once you sit down to watch the show, have you ever looked at the two sides of the stage? Two "busts" adorn the stage.

LEFT: This billboard of another dancer can be found in front of The Golden Horseshoe.

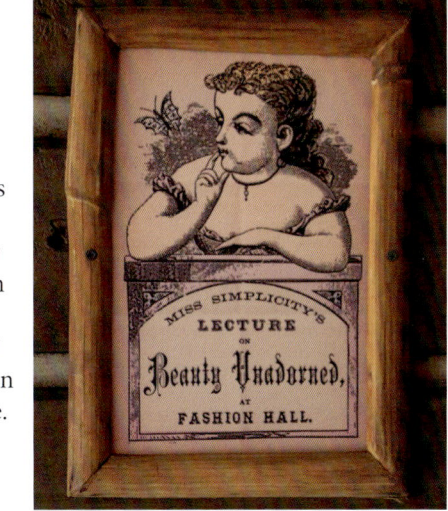

ABOVE: Miss Simplicity in a shoulder-less dress can be seen on the front porch of Pooh's Corner.

BELOW RIGHT: The lively poster of Lotta the Miners (sic) Darling can be seen on the Gold Nugget Dance Hall in Rainbow Ridge, on Big Thunder Mountain Railroad. It is on the last building, just as you turn right towards the station. If you are standing outside of the attraction, between the entrance and Rancho del Zocalo Restaurante, look at the building to the left of the tracks that lead to the train storage area.

BELOW LEFT: On Pirates of the Caribbean, as you pass from the burning city to the final battle scene, make sure to look up to see this painting hanging from the rafters. It's not well lit and hard to see, but next time check it out.

ABOVE: As you walk into Fowler's Harbor, look above and to the left of the Fowler's Inn sign. You will see a figure of a lady standing on a small ledge.

LEFT: A closer look reveals that she is flashing a little ankle. Very un-lady like, but right in line for a bar maid with sailors and pirates for customers.

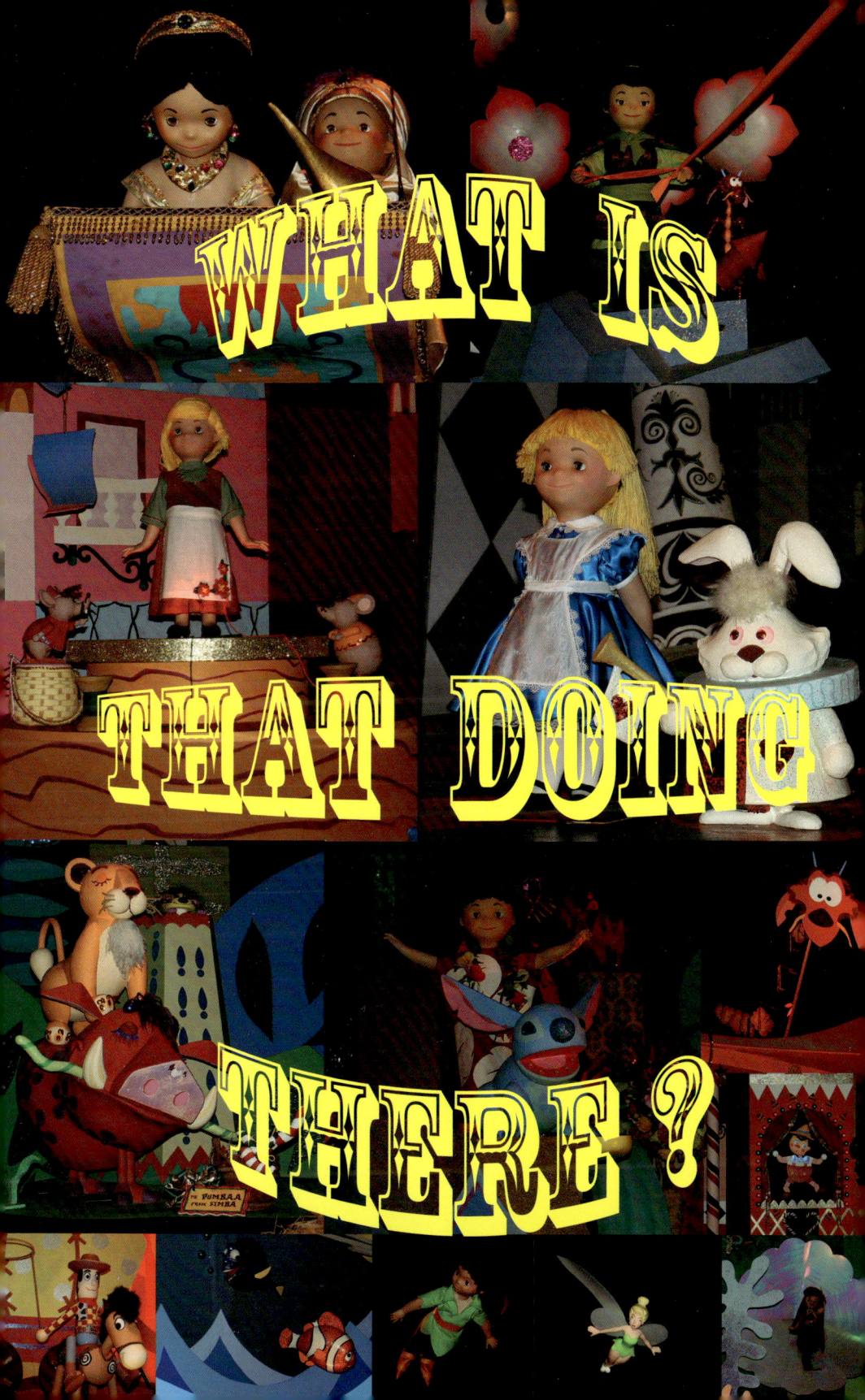

ABOVE AND LEFT: One of the most beloved attractions at Disneyland is the Walt Disney's Enchanted Tiki Room. Some of my favorite characters are the Tiki Drummers. As a kid, I always looked forward to that part. Well, it seems one of these little guys escaped and made his way over to the Tropical Imports stand in front of Jungle Cruise. He can be seen by looking up or when in the upstairs queue for Jungle Cruise.

LEFT: In the upper queue of Jungle Cruise, you can get a much better look at the Tiki Drummer.

PREVIOUS PAGE: During the 2008 re-furb, thirty Disney characters were added to it's a small world. It is a wonderful addition to a classic attraction.
(EN: 289)

ABOVE: After you pass the hippo pool on the Jungle Cruise, you come to a jungle village. As you are passing the village, look behind the dancers. You will see a shield leaning against a village hut. There is a portrait of a lion on it. Not surprising for a village in Africa, except if you look closely, it is actually the symbol for the stage production of *The Lion King*. (EN: 159)

LEFT: A close up view of the shield with *The Lion King* symbol on it.

RIGHT: Next time you walk through Tarzan's Treehouse, watch for these guys. Yep, Mrs. Potts and Chip from *Beauty and the Beast* can be seen at the end of the attraction. When you get back to ground level, you see the research and cooking area. Look in the second area where all the pots and pans are, and you just might see them.

LEFT: In my first book, I used a picture of this pirate to show who my choice for a caricature of Walt Disney might be. Pirates of the Caribbean is always going through maintenance, and as a result, some of the pirates get restless and move from time to time.

ABOVE AND LEFT: Since that time, the Red Head has received a new pirate guard. They are wearing the same clothes, but this pirate doesn't look as mean and scheming as the last one. In fact, he looks like he may have run up to Club 33 to get some rum, grog, or perhaps both from the lounge. Perhaps he's just sleepy.

ABOVE: Have you ever really looked at the emblem on the uniforms of the Little Green Men (LGM)? Next time you are on Buzz Lightyear Astro Blasters, stop and look at the emblem. You might be surprised. It may even make you a little hungry.

BELOW: On closer inspection, it looks suspiciously like a pepperoni and mushroom pizza. Some people think it is a nod to Redd Rockett's Pizza Port in Tomorrowland. However, it is actually a nod to Pizza Planet, the restaurant where the LGM's claw machine is located in the film. The restaurant's logo also has a similar Saturn pizza logo. But, why did PIXAR include the pizza logo in the movie in the first place? The PIXAR folks are also famous for putting nods to things in their past or that they like. Could this be a popular pizza for the production crew? Your guess is as good as mine. (EN: 80 / 81)

LEFT: In the court yard of the Princess Fantasy Faire, between the entrance and the exit of the Princess Meet and Greet, you will see Clopin's Music Box. As you turn the wheel on the front, it plays music and the people of the village dance (or move up and down). Wait, the people of the village? Take a closer look at the people of the village. (EN: 259)

BELOW: As you look closer at the people of the village, you will see familiar faces. There's Belle and the Beast (in human form, *Beauty and the Beast*), Smee (*Peter Pan*), Geppetto (*Pinocchio*), Doc (*Snow White and the Seven Dwarfs*), and more. How many can you spot?

ABOVE: When you enter the Mad Hatters in Fantasyland, look for this mirror hanging above the cash registers. It is wonderfully detailed with the Caterpillar from *Alice in Wonderland* asking "Who-R-U?". The mirror may appear to be an ordinary mirror but keep looking and you will see another familiar *Alice in Wonderland* face. The Cheshire Cat will begin to smile at you. Oh, and in case you are wondering why there is a genie bottle, that is actually the Caterpillar's Hookah.

BELOW: Take a closer look at the Cheshire Cat's face in the mirror. He has that classic crescent moon smile, and a little mischief in his eyes.

QUIZ: Do you remember the Caterpillar's name? You may think that it is Mr. Caterpillar, but that is what Alice called the White Rabbit, "Mr. Rabbit! Wait!". (Answer EN: 242)

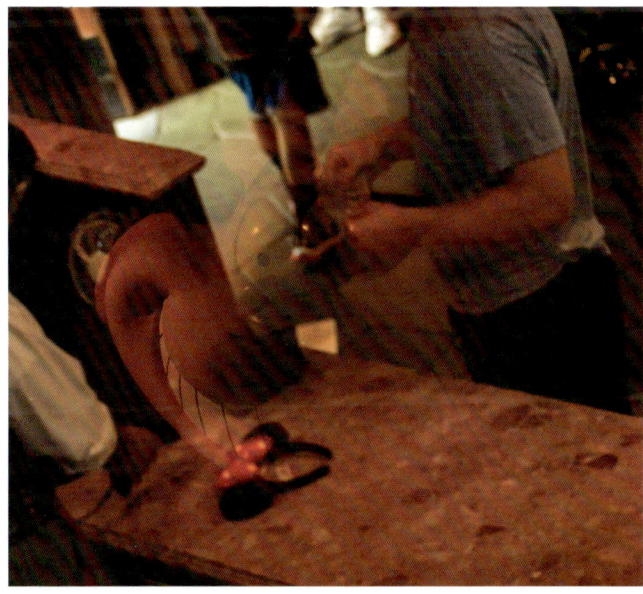

ABOVE: Next time you ride Mr. Toad's Wild Ride, watch for the weasels. This is the mural in the indoor queue area, which shows Guests what to expect. Take a closer look at the warehouse in the upper left corner.

BELOW: There you will see three weasels. What are the *Who Framed Roger Rabbit* weasels doing here, you ask? Well actually, the main villains in the *Wind in the Willows* are also weasels. So they actually do belong here. So why do they look a lot like the weasels from *Who Framed Roger Rabbit* They served as the inspiration for the weasels featured in *Who Framed Roger Rabbit*. (EN: 287)

ABOVE: After busting out of the fire place and re-entering Toad Hall, you will see two more weasels hanging from the chandeliers. As you continue through the attraction, you will continue to see weasels in the bar, courtroom, and more.

QUIZ: As long as we are talking about weasels, can you name the five *Who Framed Roger Rabbit* weasels (Answer EN: 152)

Quiz: Bonus question. Why is there no question mark at the end of the *Who Framed Roger Rabbit* movie title? (Answer EN: 297)

BELOW: As you pass the Constabulary (Police Station, for those of you not from England), look at the upstairs window. That sure looks like Sherlock Holmes.

SOUNDS?
In a picture book?
That's Just Crazy Talk!

BELOW: Have you ever stood on the Big Thunder Trail bridge and watched the trains of Big Thunder Mountain Railroad go by? It's a great place to stop, relax, enjoy the view, and the sounds. If you listen as the train starts down the grade, you can often hear the train's whistle blowing in a great panic, having just escaped the explosions. But, look carefully at the train engines next time.

BELOW: There's a bell, but no whistle on the engine. Where is that sound coming from? None of the engines have a whistle, although there is one in the station. The sound is not coming from that direction. Could it be a "g-g-g-g-g-g Ghost Whistle"?
(EN: 71)

ABOVE AND LEFT: I mentioned in the Urban Legends chapter that this is not a left over tunnel from Mine Train Through Nature's Wonderland. However, there is something special about this tunnel today. If you get close to the fence and listen carefully, you can here miners talking and working in the tunnel.

Prior to Critter Country, the land was known as Bear Country. The Country Bear Jamboree was playing where The Many Adventures of Winnie the Pooh is installed. During the show, you could hear, but never see, a bear named Rufus who ran the show. That was not the only place you could hear Rufus. As you entered the land, you could hear Rufus snoring up in his cave on the left. When Splash Mountain was added, and the land renamed, a tribute to Rufus was installed.

ABOVE: Although not the original sound track, you can still hear snoring coming from the house that replaced Rufus' cave.

BELOW: Want to hear the snoring really well? Then you might have to get a little wet and ride Splash Mountain. You can be hear it best at the end of the u-turn just before the first small drop called Slippin' Falls. The house is labeled Brer Bear (sic). (EN: 253)

ABOVE AND RIGHT: Many people don't realize that much of Tarzan's Treehouse is a hands-on experience, including bells to ring, a xylophone to play, pots and pans to bang, ropes to climb and many other things.

LEFT: Have you ever looked up at the fantastic clock sitting on top of Toontown's City Hall? Next time you are in Toontown on the hour, watch the City Hall clock. It puts on quite the little show. (EN: 184)

ABOVE AND RIGHT: Have you ever stopped to use the drinking fountain at the Toontown Gas Station? One is designed for little kids and one is designed for bigger "kids". Go ahead and use them. You may hear some hilarity. Oh, and if you use them in the evening before the land closes for the fireworks, you might see some wonderful colors. (EN: 180 / 186)

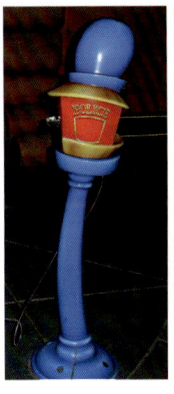

ABOVE, RIGHT AND FAR RIGHT: Whenever walking around Toontown, be sure to knock on doors, pick-up phones, push door bells, and try everything to see what fun and interesting sounds the Imagineers have created for you. Remember, Toontown is a hands on, interactive play area for kids. (EN: 185)

Sounds have always played an important part of Disneyland; from the back ground music on Main Street, shops, and restaurants, to the marvelous scores on the attractions. Here are a few sounds that you may have never seen, ahhh, really heard before.

The old telephones in the Starbucks have been there since 1974, when the location was called The Market House. I was very excited to learn that they had survived the 2014 re-furbishment. If you pick up any of the ear pieces from the telephones, you will hear what a real, turn-of-the-century (1900's not 2000's) party line call sounded like. It's fun, try it. (EN: 161)

ABOVE: These two phones can be found just inside the front door.

LEFT: This phone is located just inside the front side door off Center Street.

RIGHT: This phone is located in the rear of the store near the rear door off Center Street.

Speaking of old fashion crank phones, have you seen the one in the Main Street Magic Shop? When you talk about magic, you have to talk about Houdini. In addition to being a great escape artist, Houdini spent much of his time debunking mediums. He would attend séances, to observe how the medium was tricking the audience, and then expose them.

He even made a public challenge for anyone to prove they could communicate with the dead. If you pick up the ear piece of the phone and listen, you will hear an actual recording of Houdini making one of his famous challenges: to pay $1,000 to anyone who could prove that he could breathe while performing his underwater escape act. (EN: 153 / 158)

LEFT: The phone is located in the small access hall to the 20th Century Music Company.

RIGHT: A front view of the phone.

ABOVE: A close up of the plaque giving credit to David Copperfield's International Museum and Library of the Conjuring Arts for providing the recording of Houdini.

ABOVE: As you are walking down Main Street, towards the Castle, you will find Center Street about half way down. Turn right and you will find many more wonderful details and tribute windows here.

BELOW BOTH: One of my favorite tribute windows is for Bob Gurr. He is a genius with all things wheeled. There is a famous saying about Bob that if it has wheels at Disneyland, it was probably designed by Bob. That explains why his window is themed as a bicycle shop.

RIGHT: Closer look at the window.

ABOVE, RIGHT AND BELOW: While admiring Bob Gurr's window, look to the right and you will see a window advertising piano lessons. This window is not a tribute window, but has its own special surprise. If you listen, you will notice that this window, and two others, has sounds coming from it. For this window, you will hear a teacher instructing someone how to play the piano and the student playing the piano.

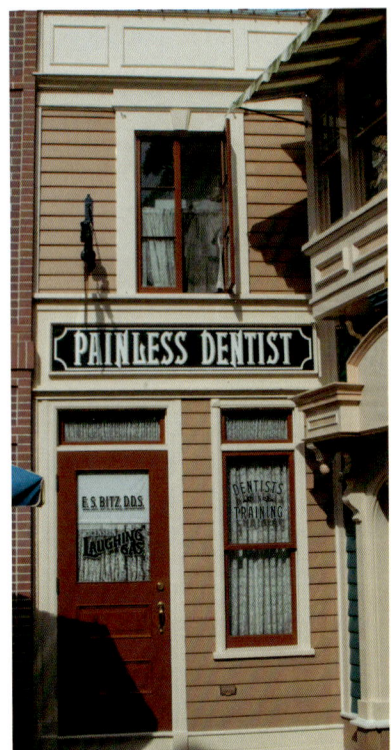

ABOVE AND ABOVE RIGHT: Look to the right of the piano lesson window and there is a window advertising "Painless Dentistry". You'll hear the dentist, his drill, and a patient. From the sound of things, there may be some false advertising going on.

RIGHT: Now turn around, and you will see Hotel Marceline. This is a tribute to the town of Marceline, MO. Walt Disney spent several years of his youth growing up in Maceline and had many fond memories of the town. This town reportedly inspired much of Disneyland including Main Street U.S.A. and the original Tom Sawyer Island. If you listen carefully, you can hear one of the guests taking a bath, but don't peek.

ABOVE: Crime? In Disneyland? Well, not really, but even Toon Town needs a detective once in a while. This business can be found on Center Street, to the right of Hotel Marceline. Stop by and listen to what this detective is investigating.

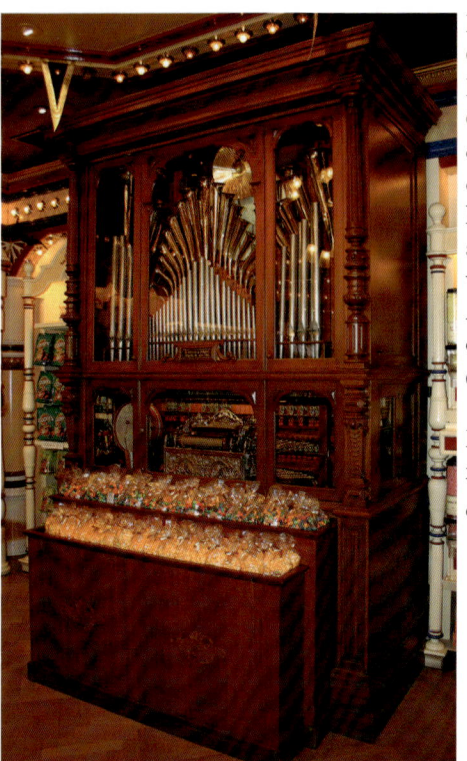

LEFT: This beautiful 1907 Welte, Style 4 Concert Orchestrion sits in the rear of the Penny Arcade which shares space with the Candy Shoppe. Many people think it is an organ, but it is much more. If you take a closer look, you will see it has strings, horns, and even a drum. It is often now surrounded, or at least partially covered, with display stands. And yes, it still works. As the sign says, it has 265 pipes and "It is currently playing 75 key Welte roll music."
(EN: 171 / 172 / 174)

BELOW: This Orchestrion has played music for the Penny Arcade since opening day at Disneyland.

BELOW: The Orchestrion is a beautiful and wonderful musical instrument. It is well maintained by Disneyland Cast Members. The brass pipes are all functional and the wood is beautiful. It plays songs at set intervals, and even plays holiday music during the Christmas season.

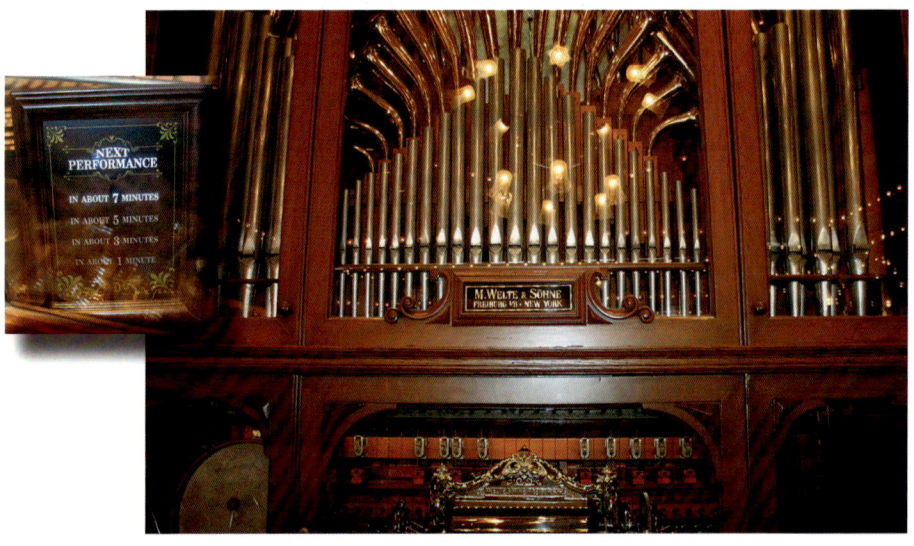

ABOVE AND BELOW: Have you every really looked at the little circus tent building to the rear of Dumbo the Flying Elephant? This building houses a wonderful looking Gavioli Band Organ, circa 1915. This instrument is capable of being heard up to half a mile away and recreating the sounds of several band instruments. When Disneyland first opened, it was located more towards the center of Fantasyland and was responsible for the area music.

After the 1983 remodel, it was moved to its current location and used for the theme music for Dumbo. Though it is no longer operational, it used to play several of the Guests' favorite tunes while Dumbo took them for a flight. The music played now during the attraction is pre-recorded.

(EN: 82 / 83 / 84 / 119)

ABOVE: Just before you enter Snow White's Scary Adventure, you will see this brass book and apple to the left. It reads:

"The Poison Apple
With the Apple
Snow White
Fell Into A
Death-Like Sleep
From An Evil Spell"

"BEWARE!
A Touch Of This Apple
Stirs A Torrent
Of Fright...
Unleashing
The Crys
Of Evil's Delight"

LEFT: Many people touch the book as they walk by or read the book. Have you ever touched the apple? Go ahead, touch the apple to hear the Evil Queen. (EN: 72)

In 1983, Disneyland had actress Adriana Castelotti make a new recording of the song, "I'm Wishing", from *Snow White and the Seven Dwarfs*. This song can be

heard at the well, and reportedly, all over the Park after hours, when everything is quiet. In addition, all those coins that Guests toss in for their wishes are donated to local children's charities. This sentiment is shared by the words carved next to the pulley, "Your Wishes Will Help...Children Everywhere". (EN: 251 / 208)

Gone, But Still There

Or, More Ghosts of Disneyland Attractions Past

One of the more well-known extinct attractions in Disneyland history is Monsanto's House of the Future. This house was built completely out of plastic and featured many household amenities we take for granted today. These included flat screen televisions and microwave ovens. When it came time for its removal, construction crews brought in a wreaking ball to knock it down. Unfortunately, the ball merely bounced off. Eventually, it was decided to bring in chain saws and crowbars to take the House of the Future apart, piece by piece. You might think that was the end of this attraction. While true for the most part, you can still see a small, but critical, piece of the House of the Future. As you walk up to the queue for the Pixie Hollow meet and greet, look to your left. You'll notice a lot of plants in a large green planter box. Take another look. That was actually the foundation of the House of the Future. (EN: 239)

ABOVE: Model of Disneyland, located at The Walt Disney Family Museum in San Francisco's Presidio. The model is based on the "fun map" concept that used to be sold at Disneyland. The House of the Future is located in the center, and basically shows how it looked, its approximate location, and orientation. (EN: 239)

RIGHT: A closer look at the model and the unique shape of the House of the Future.

Author's Note: Want to learn more about Walt Disney, his life, the company he created, and his projects? Then the Walt Disney Family Museum is a must visit location for you

ABOVE: Look left as you are walking up to the queue.

BELOW: Look behind the sign post. See the green concrete foundation now partially covered with netting? That is the original foundation for the House of the Future.

LEFT: As you pass the sign post, look left into the bushes. You will see the green concrete box.

LEFT: If you look into the bushes behind the sign post, you will see more of the foundation.

RIGHT: To the right of Pixie Hollow's exit is a walkway that leads back to the entrance. Just after you enter the walkway, look to your left for this grassy area. This is the top of the foundation where the House of the Future sat. You can see it is now filled in with dirt, planted grass and a tree.

ABOVE: Prior to Dumbo the Flying Elephant, Chicken of the Sea Pirate Ship and Restaurant and a large rock formation called Skull Rock were the neighbors to the left of Storybook Land. They were completely removed as part of the 1983 Fantasyland re-furbishment. Or were they? The rocks just to the left of Monstro are leftovers from this large rock formation. The rocks just out of this picture to the left are all new rocks, including the ponds. (EN: 222 /223 / 234)

LEFT: A closer look at the rock outcropping that was left. This upright, flat top rock can be seen in many vintage pictures when Skull Rock was still present.

RIGHT: In addition to the small rock outcropping next to Monstro, the plant covered rocks above him are also left over from Skull Rock. However, they are next to impossible to see today with the plant coverings.

AUTHOR'S NOTE: This restaurant was also known as Pirate Ship Restaurant and Captain Hook's Galley.

ABOVE AND LEFT: Sitting in front of Mr. Toad's Wild Ride is a ride vehicle. It is there as a photo opp, so people do not hold up the queue when loading.

Most people probably just think it is just one of the current ride vehicles that was taken out of service. This is actually an original ride vehicle that was retired when the larger vehicles were brought from The Magic Kingdom's Mr. Toad Wild Ride to replace them. (EN: 309)

As I've mentioned in previous chapters, the Country Bear Jamboree is one of the most popular extinct attractions. The attraction was originally conceived to be part of the Mineral King Ski Resort that Walt Disney was planning. After Walt's death, The Walt Disney Company attempted to continue with the Walt's idea, but eventually canceled the project and shelved the ideas. As they say in Imagineering, no good idea ever goes away. The attraction was taken off the shelf and built at the Magic Kingdom in Walt Disney World. It was so popular that plans were immediately started to add it to Disneyland.

In 1972, the Indian Village was removed and Bear Country was added. The Country Bear Jamboree ran from March 1972 until it went into hibernation in September 2001. The attraction went through several changes and additions over the years, such as the Country Bear Christmas Special and the Country Bear Vacation Hoedown. After the attraction closed, most of the characters and scenery were taken to Walt Disney World to help support its operation. That is, except for three stowaways that stayed behind. They can be seen in the previous edition of my book. There are three other parts of the attraction that can still be seen. (EN: 61/62)

ABOVE: The bridge that Guests use today to access the queue for Winnie the Pooh is the same one used for Country Bear Jamboree all those years ago. The Imagineers obviously changed the signage and repainted it, removed the small signs and lights on each side, and changed the two hanging lights on the eves. A clock and a wait time was also added. Other than that, it is the same bridge. (EN: 63)

ABOVE This is the location of the original entrance into the theaters. A comparison of the current entrance to historical pictures of the entrance to the Country Bear Jamboree shows a remarkable similarity between the two from the top of the door up. However, the lower portion is very different. It appears that the entrance was rebuilt and moved out a few feet. Even so, it definitely has the same aesthetic as the original entrance.

BELOW: The exit to The Many Adventures of Winnie the Pooh was the original exit for the Country Bears Jamboree. Again, it's been re-themed a little. (EN: 70)

BELOW: On July 4, 1962, The Indian Trading Post was added to the Indian Village. Even after the 1972 change from Indian Village to Bear Country, it remained The Indian Trading Post until the 1988 re-theme of the area to Critter Country. Disneyland decided to change the Indian Trading Post to the Briar Patch. This kept in theme with Splash Mountain, the newest attraction at the time. The Indian Trading post sold "Authentic Indian Crafts". Today, the Briar Patch mainly sells hats. (EN: 64)

ABOVE: Close up of The Briar Patch sign.

RIGHT: Outside, the roof has grass and other plants growing on it. If you go into the store and look up, you will see some treats for Br'er Rabbit growing down into the building

RIGHT: A well-known extinct attraction was Mine Train Though Nature's Wonderland. This attraction ran from July 2, 1956 until January 2, 1977. It was replaced by Big Thunder Mountain Railroad. As part of the Mine Train, there was a two-story building that housed a store just to the right known as Mineral Hall. The general area was known as El Zocalo. Many Guests enjoyed the glowing rocks and water of Rainbow Caverns so much, they wanted their own. Mineral Hall sold rocks, minerals, and black lights to Guests. Many of the rocks you could buy would fluoresce, or glow, under a black light, making it possible for Guests to take a little bit of the Rainbow Caverns experience home with them. Mineral Hall was closed in 1962 and replaced with Casa de Fritos. The upstairs is currently closed to Guests, but downstairs is still in use today as part of Rancho del Zocalo Restaurante. The restaurante uses this part of the building for desserts and the cash registers. (EN: 66 / 96 / 246 / 248)

BELOW: The building with the star on top was the former Mineral Hall. The building to the right was the one-story Assay Office, and was eventually converted to a two-story building, but kept the general look of its unique top. The two windows installed in the second story were originally located where the double doors are now. The wording has since been re-furbished. They now serve as a tribute to Mineral Hall. (EN: 247 / 250)

Many of the original rock formations from the Mine Train still exist at Disneyland. As you walk on Big Thunder Trail, the large rock formation in front of Big Thunder Ranch and Big Thunder Barbecue was a part of the rock formations used in the Mine Train.
(EN:157)

ABOVE: This is the view of the rock formation as you walk from Frontierland to Fantasyland. On the left, you can see the entrance to Big Thunder Ranch.

LEFT: A closer look at the large rock formation to the right of the petting area. This formation would tower over Guests as they rode the Mine Trains.

QUIZ: As we learned in the OK, A Few More Hidden Mickeys chapter, officially all rides are called attractions with the exception Mr. Toad's Wild Ride. There are actually two attractions that can be referred to as rides. The other does not have the word ride in its title. Can you name that attraction?
(Answer EN: 65)

ABOVE: As you continue to walk towards Fantasyland, you will notice a large rock archway just beyond the peak on the previous page. This is the archway that you see in many of the historical photographs and films of the Mine Train. The archway is now partially obscured by trees on each side.

LEFT: You can get a better view of the archway if you pass it and look back. This would have been the back side of the arch that Guests riding the Mine Train would pass by.

RIGHT: This view can be seen if you walk into Big Thunder Ranch Barbecue, and look back. This would have been the more common view for Guests during the Mine Train days.

141

LEFT: As I mentioned in the Urban Legends chapter, the big cave on the backside of Big Thunder Mountain Railroad is not original. If you walk into Big Thunder Ranch Barbecue, you can find some more original rock formations and one of the two old tunnels that still exist. Walk back to the stage and look right and you'll see an entryway for Cast Members performing or accessing the kitchen. Look at the base of the rocks and you will see the top of an archway. This is actually the top of one of the original tunnels. The grade of the area was changed during construction, leaving only the top of the tunnel visible. This tunnel led to the off stage storage area for the Mine Trains. (EN: 67)

BELOW: A closer look at the top of the tunnel.

ABOVE: Just to the left of the wooden fence is where the old tunnel from the previous page is located. The rock formation to the right is all original.

BELOW: If you continue looking to the right, the rock formation eventually leads up to the Cast Member host shack for Big Thunder Ranch Barbecue.

NOTE: If you continue walking up Big Thunder Trail, just before you enter Fantasyland, there is a large gate on your right. Behind that gate is where the second original tunnel is still located. Unfortunately, unless a Cast Member is using the gate, you will not be able to see that tunnel. You have to look down as the top of the tunnel is all that remains.

ABOVE: Panoramic view of the Big Thunder Trail rock formation that was formerly part of Mine Train Through Nature's Wonderland.

ABOVE AND LEFT: In between the Pirate's Lair on Tom Sawyer Island loading area and Fowler's Harbor is a lonely, old loading dock. This dock is currently used as one of the three designated smoking areas in the Park. Between December 1955 and May 1997, this dock was used for the Mike Fink Keel Boats. (EN: 215)

LEFT AND BELOW LEFT: Prior to becoming part of River Belle Terrace, this section of the restaurant was known as The Silver Banjo BBQ. It was open from 1957 to 1961 and owned by actor Don DeFore. Just below the crown moulding was a large Banjo sign. Look closely and you can see a cap that covers the power box used by the sign.
(EN: 225 / 226 / 227)

ABOVE: As you pass the Astro Orbitor and enter Tomorrowland, have you noticed the very futuristic walls on the front of Buzz Lightyear Astro Blasters and Star Tours - The Adventure Continues? They did a great job theming these walls to match these fun attractions. Or did they? These walls were actually installed during the 1967 Tomorrowland re-furb. They were so well-themed to the land, that they have been kept to this day. They have gone through a couple of color changes over the years, but otherwise have been left as is from the day they were installed. (EN: 216/ 217 / 218 / 219 / 220)

LEFT: The walls were originally colored silver. In 1998, they were given a golden tone to match the rest of Tomorrowland's golden bronze look. (EN: 221)

ABOVE: The wall in front of Buzz Lightyear as it appears today.

BELOW: The wall in front of Star Tours as it appears at night.

ABOVE: When Disneyland first opened, there were no credit cards. If people wanted to buy something while on vacation, they paid with cash. If people needed more money or other bank services, there was a full service Bank of America located on Main Street U.S.A., where Disneyana is located today. You could even open a new account. In addition, it was one of very few banks that was open on Sundays and holidays. Bank of America sponsored the bank until 1992. After that, it was simply known as Bank of Main Street until 2001, when it became an Annual Pass Holder service center. The building was converted to the Disneyana store in 2009. (EN: 313).

LEFT: If you go along the right side of the Disneyana store, towards the restrooms, you will see this mural as a tribute to the bank that was once here.

RIGHT: You may have noticed the safe and thought it was just a prop or actually used for storing the fine art. It was the actual working safe when it was a bank. Take a look at the mechanics of it next time you are there. They are as beautiful as they are functional.

People are familiar with the names of the more popular characters, such as Mickey Mouse and Goofy. They are even familiar with some of the supporting characters having names, such as Br'er Fox, or attraction characters, like "The Redhead". However, many of the other characters around the Park that you wouldn't think have names actually do. Some are official, but just not publicized. Many are given names by Cast members so they can easily referenced amongst themselves. And some are even given names by Guests.

RIGHT: One character that anyone who has been on Jungle Cruise will be familiar with is Trader Sam. He can be seen at the end of the Jungle Cruise plying his trade. He's been having a limited time sale of two of his heads for one of yours. Trader Sam has become such a popular character that there is a bar at the Disneyland Hotel named after him. It is a fun and well-themed bar, but there is none of his wife's stew.

AUTHOR'S NOTE: The name tag on the prior page is a graphic created by the author and should <u>not</u> be interpreted to be an endorsement by or any affiliation with Disneyland or The Disney Company.

ABOVE: In this view, you can see Trader Sam with his little elephant side kick. The elephant's name is Squirt.

BELOW: As you ride Jungle Cruise, one of the more famous scenes is the elephant bathing pool; especially the big elephant taking a shower in the water fall. Her name is Bertha. Check her out next time. And don't worry, she does have her trunks on.

RIGHT: When the original Fantasmic Dragon was being made, her code name was Dymo, but Cast Members and Guests affectionately began calling her Bucky. She performed until 2009. After retirement, she went on tour, and was seen at the D23 exhibit at the Ronald Reagan Presidential Library. This picture is from that display. (EN: 169)

After Bucky's retirement, she was replaced by a new dragon code named Snaps McGee. Cast Members and Guests began calling her Murphy, possibly in reference to Murphy's Law. This is reportedly due to the malfunctions when Murphy made her first appearances. . (EN: 170)

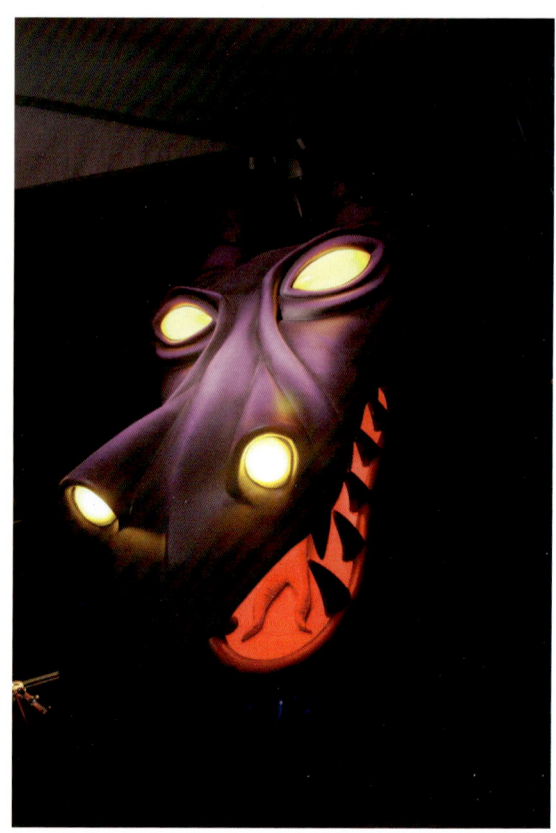

ABOVE: Murphy in the final battle scene with Mickey Mouse.

RIGHT: Murphy as she makes her first dramatic appearance in the show.

ABOVE: If your child says they are scared of the Abominable Snow Man when you go to ride the Matterhorn Bobsleds, just say, "Who, Harold? He's not scary." (EN: 168)

BELOW: Next time you are walking on the south side of the Matterhorn (across from the Sleeping Beauty Castle restrooms) look for this plaque of Harold's foot print. It's just inside the fence line.

As you walk down Main Street U.S.A. towards Sleeping Beauty Castle, you will pass the Main Street Cinema. The theater shows classic silent Disney cartoons on a continuous loop. It's a nice, cool place to rest on a hot, busy day. Note: Standing room only.

ABOVE: The quiet ticket seller is Tilly. She sits patiently waiting for Guests. Take a closer look at her name badge. She is from Marceline, MO, another tribute to Walt Disney's boyhood town. Now Tilly doesn't move a whole lot, but she does keep up with the seasons. She is wearing her green Holiday outfit.

ABOVE RIGHT: A closer look at Tilly's Name Badge.

RIGHT: Here Tilly is dressed in her Halloween best.

LEFT: Tilly in her spring outfit.

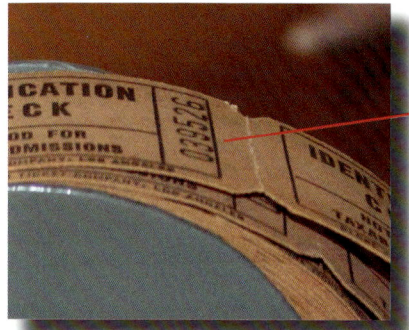

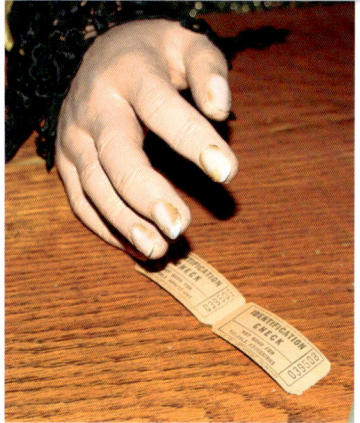

Are they "boo boos" or planned Easter Eggs by the Imagineers? Every so often, you will find something that makes you say, "That's strange." I think they are planned, as this one comes and goes.

ABOVE RIGHT: Note the ticket number is 039526.

ABOVE LEFT: That ticket is on top, and there are three additional tickets ahead of it on the spool. That means the last ticket handed out should be 039521.

LEFT: But the tickets she is handing out right now are 039509 and 039508.

ABOVE: You can see the next ticket in this picture is 039521.

RIGHT: The ticket sitting on the counter that she just handed out is 039509.

This was eventually corrected, but keep your eye out for more, like Oogie's Holiday Trick And Treats wheel of fortune. Take a look at the characters on it in Chapter 13.

155

LEFT AND ABOVE: This one you would think would be easy, given that her name is printed across the front of her cabinet. Well maybe not. I've asked people if they want their fortune told by Esmeralda, only to be told they never noticed that the fancy writing on the glass spelled out her name.

BELOW: Next time you are there, take a look at the cards she is using to tell Guests' fortunes. They are actually Haunted Mansion cards, depicting the four portraits in the stretching room. (EN: 181)

ABOVE: This beautifully costumed chief has been watching over his village and the Rivers of America for years. He was affectionately known as "Chief Waves-A-Lot", as he is constantly waving at all the passer-by on the river and trains. Today, he if often simply referred to as The Chief. (EN: 179)

Have you ever been to City Hall at Disneyland? Many wonderful services are provided there, including Guest Services, free button distribution (Happy Birthday, Just Married, Anniversary, First Visit, I'm Celebrating, and more), Guest compliments for Cast Members, phone call from Mickey Mouse for your birthday, and much more. The one service we all hope to never use is when a parent gets lost. City Hall is clearly marked as a location children can come to find their lost parents.

ABOVE: Lost Parent signs sit on each side of the front porch of City Hall.

LEFT: Take a closer look at the parents on the sign. Why they look familiar? They are Mr. and Mrs. Darling, the parents of Wendy, John, and Michael from *Peter Pan*. (EN: 178)

RIGHT: This map is mounted on the Penny Machine on the porch of Pooh's Corner. You may might be saying it's a typical map of the Hundred Acre Woods. Possibly, but look at the compass headings. Instead of North, West, East, and South; we have P, O, O, and H. What does that spell? POOH!

LEFT: There are many wonderful sites, gags, and things to do in Toontown. As you enter Toontown, look for this sign on your right. Like any other town, they have marked important landmarks. This one is number 3, wait for it, and 1/2? Yep, leave it to the toons to have a half. They have never been good with numbers.

This one marks the date when people were allowed into Toontown to enjoy all its wonders, or at least "Some Important Date".

The town's motto is actually pretty nice: "Laughter Is Sunshine You Can Hear".

ABOVE: As you walk through Minnie Mouse's house in Toontown, there are many wonderful things for you and your children to see and play with. Have you ever noticed that there are some things for adults too? Take a look a Minnie's refrigerator. There are fun notes and pictures to look at. Did you notice the recipe hanging from the pink heart?

RIGHT: It is a recipe for Minnie Mouse's Famous Chewy Cheesy Chip Cookies. Go ahead and try it sometime.

Minnie Mouse's Famous Chewy Cheesy Chip Cookies

2/3 cup shortening
2/3 cup butter
1 cup sugar
1 cup brown sugar
2 eggs
2 tsp. Vanilla
3 cups sifted flour
1 tsp. Baking soda
1 tsp. Salt
10 oz. Semi-Sharp Cheddar Cheese Chips

Heat oven to 375°
Mix butter & shortening, sugars, eggs, vanilla.
Stir in dry ingredients.
Add Cheese Chips.
Spoon onto cookie sheet and bake for 10 minutes.

(Note: For a zesty taste treat, try Smoked Gouda Cheese Chips instead of Cheddar!)

ABOVE: The queue for Roger Rabbit's Cartoon Spin has many wonderful things to experience. Take a look at the address. That is a fun tongue twister to try. Can you say Toyboat, Toyboat, Toyboat & Picklepepper Inc. "3 times fast"? What? "Cantsay, It"?

BELOW: At the end of Roger Rabbit's Car Toon Spin, you will see the lockers for Lenny and Benny. Notice Benny's locker number? I've always wondered why toons and Toontown were always so rounded. Seems they know Pi (3.1415926536...). Perhaps I was wrong about them not being good with numbers.

Strollers are everywhere at Disneyland, which is not unseen. The Cast Members spend a lot of time corralling them to keep walkways clear for Guests. Some are just make-shift areas used by Cast Members. Others are clearly marked for Guests. In Disney's creative way, they are not your run of the mill stroller parking signs, though.

LEFT: This sign can be found at the Jedi Training Academy area. Should that Padawan have a Light Saber so soon?

RIGHT: This stroller parking sign is located at Star Tours. Man, I wish we had a hover stroller when our child was young.

Anyone who has been to Disneyland is probably familiar with the Wait Time signs throughout the Park. Have you stopped to look at the backs of the ones in Fantasyland? Several of the signs have cute sayings on the back, related to their original movies.

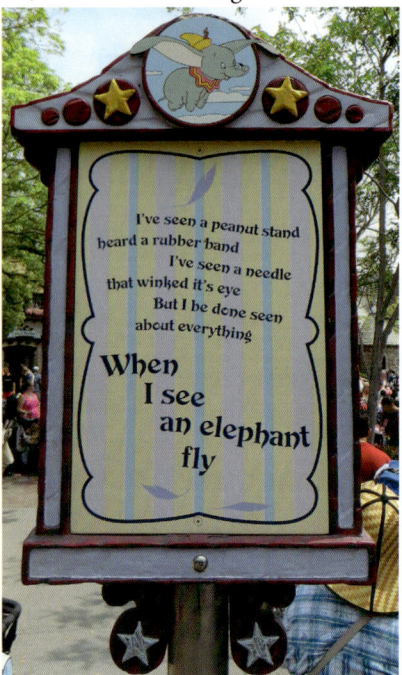

ABOVE: Dumbo The Flying Elephant - "I've seen a peanut stand, heard a rubber band, I've seen a needle that winked it's (sic) eye, but I be done seen about everything. When I see an elephant fly."

BELOW: Peter Pan's Flight - "With a sprinkling of Tinker Bell's fairy dust, away they all flew, heading for Never Land."

 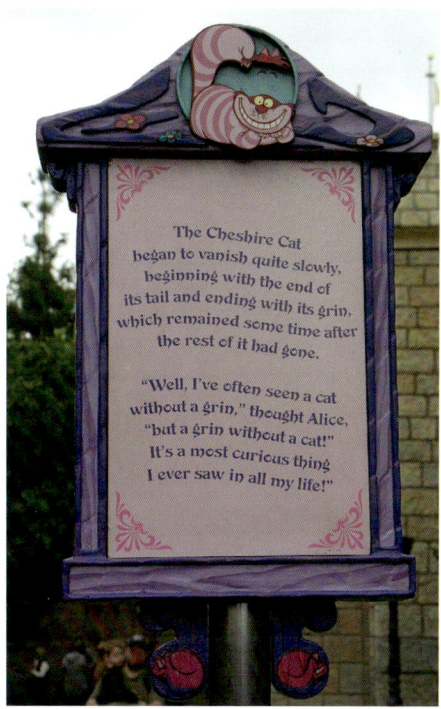

ABOVE: Alice in Wonderland - "The Cheshire Cat began to vanish quite slowly, beginning with the end of its tail and ending with its grin, which remained some time after the rest of it had gone. "Well, I've often seen a cat without a grin," thought Alice, "but a grin without a cat!" It's a most curious thing I ever saw in all my life!" (sic)

BELOW: Mr. Toad's Wild Ride - "Ho, ho! Sit still, and you shall know what driving really is, for you are in the hands of the famous, the skillful, the entirely fearless Mr. Toad!"

 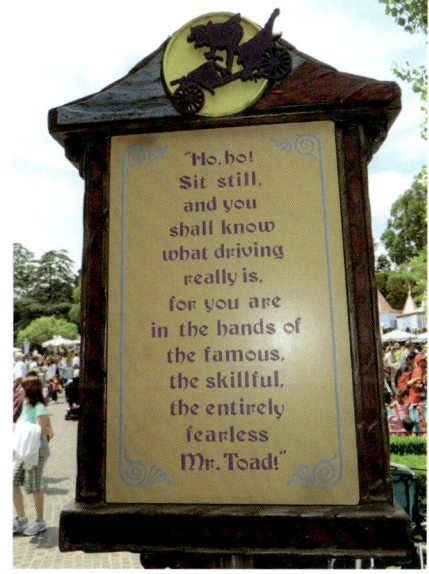

When you go to other amusement parks, do you ever notice the safety or informational signs? Probably not. If you do, they are probably just plain, little signs that you quickly ignore. Not so with Disneyland informational signs. The Imagineers took the time to theme these important signs which also help to grab your attention.

LEFT: This sign explains the Alice in Wonderland attraction and safety concerns in a beautifully decorated way.

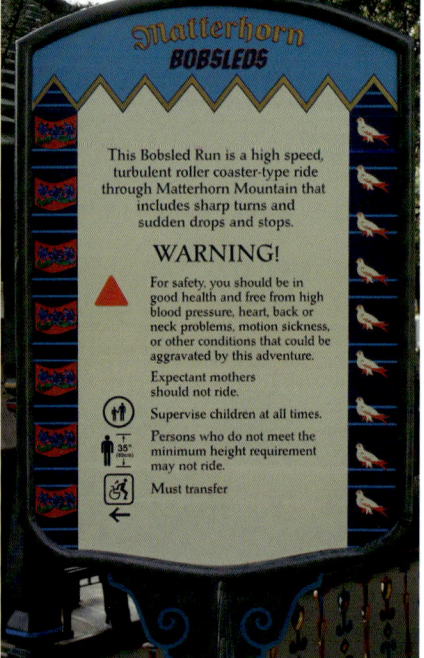

RIGHT: This warning sign for Matterhorn has a lot of information, but it gets your attention with its wonderful decorations on each side. (EN: 229)

LEFT: This is another Matterhorn sign that also gets your attention with its great design.

QUIZ TIME: As I discussed in the section on Tilly, you can sometimes find things that make you say, "That's strange." Can you spot it on this sign? See End Note for answer. (Answer EN: 230)

166

THIS PAGE: These three signs all explain where to find the compliance documents related to the operation of their attraction. They are not some ugly little sign, but are made to look like they belong where they are and still get the information across to those who are interested.

Disney was at the forefront of being eco-friendly with their green programs. Disney also tries to be in the lead for providing additional services for Guests with special needs. But, who thinks about the support animals that some of these Guests have? Disney does. In addition to care being provided for the wonderful animals at the Disneyland Kennels, Disney also provides locations for these animals to take care of other, uhhhh... duties.

LEFT: This symbol can be found on the Park guide maps to help Guests locate the dog parks. There are currently 4 dog parks in Disneyland.

BELOW: The first one of these parks I noticed is located to the right of it's a small world. The fire hydrants appear to be functional.

ABOVE: The next one I saw was this one located on Big Thunder Trail just before you enter Fantasyland. It is to your left as you are walking towards Fantasyland.

LEFT AND BELOW: This one I had to use the Park guide maps to find. It is located on the hub. You will find it between Astro Orbitors and Pixie Hollow. I've passed by this one literally thousands of times and never noticed it.

RIGHT: The last one is a small dog park in Magnolia Park, New Orleans Square between the Haunted Mansion and entrance to the Disneyland Railroad.

ABOVE: As you enter the most dangerous part of the journey on Jungle Cruise, the return to civilization, the Skipper will point out Trader Sam on your left. Have you ever looked slightly right of the front of the boat? If you have, you have seen the ad for Tropical Imports. Above and to the left of that is something written in Arabic.

BELOW: Have you ever wondered what it says? I did, so my wife asked a family friend. It says, "Oasis Family Restaurant Continuous Entertainment." Now we know. (EN: 155)

LEFT: How many of you actually listen to the Cast Members when they say 'watch your step' when loading onto the Jungle Cruise boats or 'watch your head' when loading into the submarines? This little giraffe catches your eye, entertains, and reminds you to watch your step.

RIGHT: I always dislike signs that say "KEEP OUT". They just seem rude. This sign adds that futuristic customs service feel to the mix, and softens the message, but you still know it's off limits.

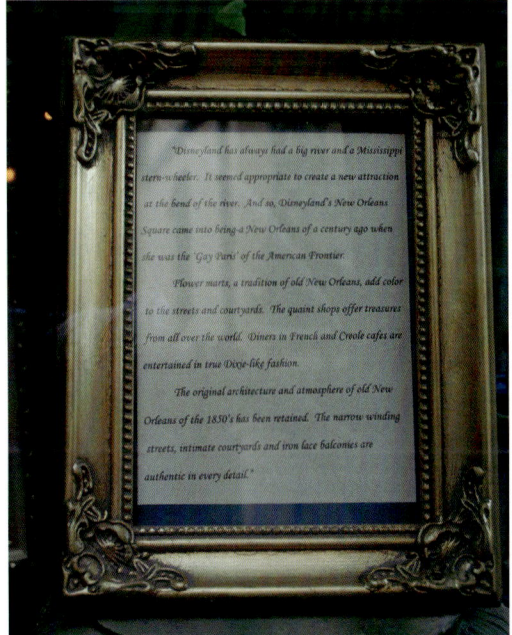

LEFT: This informational sign moves from time to time. In this picture, it is in the window directly across from the Pirates of the Caribbean exit and next to the outdoor portrait area. Ever wonder why something is the way it is in Disneyland? You can sometimes find a sign that explains it, like this one.

LEFT: If you have the first edition of my book series, then you already know about the Mouse Crossing sign on the Autopia course. Did you also happen to notice the red brick cross walk leading from the sign across the track? It really is a mouse crossing

BELOW: The red bricks lead to this mouse hole. So really, next time be cautious when passing this sign.

BELOW: When fire departments first started, they were not part of the government, whose services were available to everyone; they were private companies. You had to sign up and pay a fee for "Fire Insurance" with a company. You would then be given that company's emblem to place on the front of your building. Whenever there was a fire, all the various fire companies would respond. If they did not see their emblem on the front of your home or business, they would leave. Only the company whose emblem was displayed would stay to fight the fire. Examples of these types of emblems can be found on the various stores in New Orleans Square.

 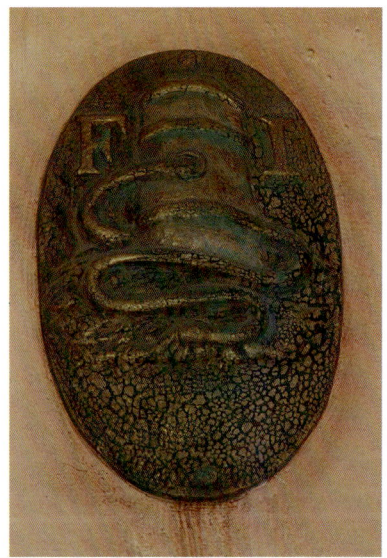

ABOVE LEFT: Cafe Orleans Restaurant. It is for the Disneyland Fire Department.

ABOVE RIGHT: Pieces of Eight gift store. It is for the F. I. Fire Department

BELOW: Le Bat en Rouge. It is the D. L. Fire Department.

ABOVE: This tree was given to Walt Disney by Bill Evans for the Park. Evans was the main landscaper during the construction of Disneyland. This tree, known as a Metasequoia, or Dawn Redwood, was once thought to be extinct. It was discovered during a pre-World War II survey by T. Kan in central China in 1941. It was re-discovered again in 1944 by T. Wang, and identified in 1946 by Professor Hu as the tree thought long extinct. A sample was given to Bill Evans, who planted it at Disneyland. (EN: 165 / 166)

PREVIOUS PAGE: This little fairy can be found in the landscaping of Pixie Hollow.

It's just a few plants, right? Well, not exactly. In addition to all the thought and coordination, there is the sheer volume. Here are the annual numbers:

a. 45,000 trees and shrubs.
b. 1 million annuals.
c. 150 landscape gardeners.
d. 10,000 flowers each time they redo the Mickey portrait at the entrance.

(EN: 272)

I talked about the Domiguez Palm Tree located next to Jungle Cruise in the first edition of my book series. Since then, I have learned another interesting fact about this tree. It is the oldest living thing at Disneyland. I began wondering if there were other Un-Seen facts about the landscaping of Disneyland.

ABOVE AND LEFT: When Walt Disney purchased the land from the Dominguez family, he promised the family the tree would not be removed. The tree had reportedly been on the property since 1896, when it was planted as a wedding present. There were other existing trees on the land, but many of them were removed as a result of a misunderstanding during construction. The trees behind city hall are another example of trees that were already on the land, but they were planted to protect the orchards that existed prior to Disneyland and were much younger than the Dominguez Palm Tree. During the 1994 re-furb of Jungle Cruise, the new queue building design was modified to accommodate the tree. The tree is still in the exact spot it was when the land was purchased. (EN: 163 /164 / 244)

While building Disneyland, Bill Evans scoured the Southern California area for older trees to be used at the Park. When he saw the white tree pictured above, he fell in love with it. He contacted the home owner who, it turns out, didn't like the tree and had planned on having it removed. He agreed to let Bill Evans remove the tree as long as he replaced it with another tree that the owner would like. The deal was struck and the Banyon tree was moved to its current location in the Jungle Cruise. Next time you enter the hippo pool, look for this great tree in the back left. (EN: 154 / 156)

ABOVE AND BELOW: The white tree you see in these three pictures is that famous Banyan tree.

THIS PAGE: Speaking of Jungle Cruise trees, during the construction of the attraction, several mature trees were needed in order to make the jungle look like it had existed for a long time. Orange trees were planted upside down to give them that "banyon tree" jungle look and feel. These trees are long since gone, but many palm trees were needed, too. Where could Bill Evans get so many mature trees? It just so happened that the new Interstate Freeway 5 was being built and all the trees in the way were being cut down. Evans made a deal with the state to remove the trees for free as long as he got to keep them to use on the Jungle Cruise. It was quite the task to stay ahead of the freeway construction, but all of the trees were removed and planted along the shores of to create a lush jungle. You can still see many of these trees today. (EN: 167)

I know that Tarzan's Treehouse is not a real tree and therefore not really landscaping. When I was a kid, and it was called Swiss Family Treehouse, I believed that it was. I think most kids still do. Besides, these are fun, so I had to include them.

Most parents are familiar with all of those steps you have to climb to make your way through Tarzan's Treehouse. Are you aware that this is not the only tree house that was built at Disneyland that you could actually go through? Can you name the others? I'll make this one easy, there are three others. The answer is on the following pages.

ABOVE: If you've ever played on Tom Sawyer Island, then the second one, Tom Sawyer's Treehouse, should have jumped to mind. This tree house sits on top of the small hill behind Lafitte's Tavern (formerly Harper's Mill). You may also know it as the stage for Fantasmic. This tree house is actually large enough to accommodate several kids at a time.

ABOVE: A closer look at the tree house.

LEFT: The third tree house is the Chip & Dale Treehouse, located in Toontown. This tree house is a very tight fit for most adults. There used to be a slide at the exit, but it was removed for safety reasons. (EN: 258)

The first three should have been pretty easy. See if you can figure out the fourth one before turning to the next page.

BELOW: Did you remember that the model home of the future in the now closed Innoventions was built in and around a tree? You see the branches on the second floor with all their electronic parts. The stairs go around part of the trunk as you walk downstairs. As you see from this picture, the trunk actually form part of the home.

BELOW: To take this full circle, I have a great little Easter egg. Have you ever stopped to look at the trunk of the smaller tree you use to enter Tarzan's Treehouse? Next time, look at the part of the trunk that is under the bridge. Some people think it looks like Grandmother Willow from *Pocahontas* or Jabba the Hut from *Star Wars*. I think both are great answers. (EN: 257)

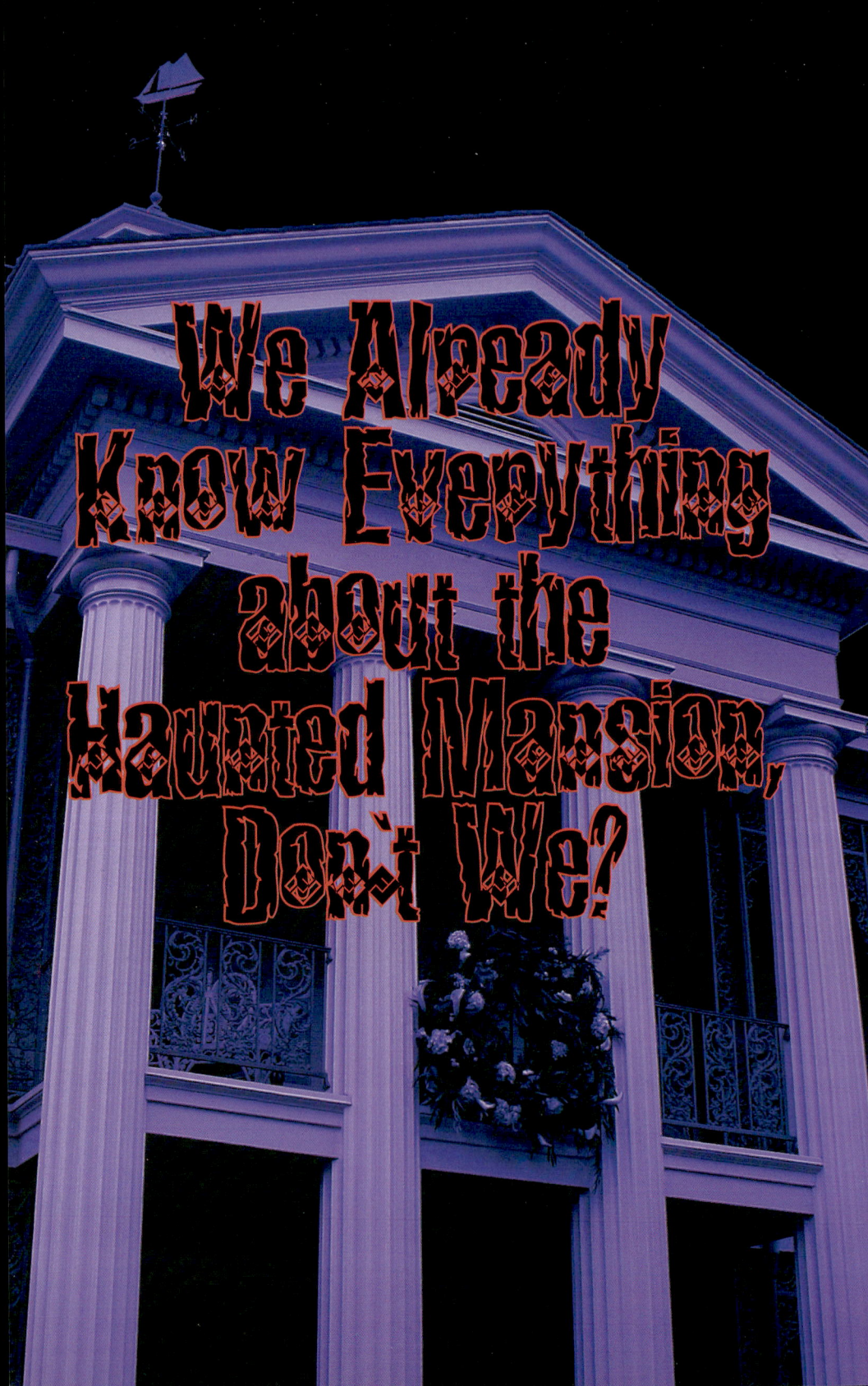

We Already Know Everything about the Haunted Mansion, Don't We?

The world famous Haunted Mansion has had so much written about it already in several outstanding books, news articles, and online. Even my previous book documented Hidden Mickeys, the Captain Nemo organ, "Roastie-Toastie" characters, and the Doom Buggies. So what could possibly be left to be seen? Not surprisingly, with the depth of skill and talent that the Imagineers put into the attraction, there is still much to be "seen".

RIGHT: Many of the streets and walk ways have been given names such as Main Street, U.S.A., Flower Street, and Center Street. The streets in New Orleans Square even have names such as Orleans Street, Front Street, and Royal Street. The street names don't actually stop at the main buildings in New Orleans Square and continue all the way to the Haunted Mansion. Outside the main entrance to the Haunted Mansion is this street sign. It indicates that Front Street runs along the Disneyland Railroad tracks and curves in front of the left side of the Haunted Mansion. The walkway that runs along the Rivers of America is called the Esplanade. This makes sense, as the definition of an esplanade is "a level, open area; especially: an area for walking or driving along a shore". (EN: 75)

BELOW AND BELOW RIGHT: Close up of the names.

As you walk through the queue of the Haunted Mansion, you will see a graveyard out front that should be familiar to everyone who has been on the attraction: a final resting place dedicated to the pets of the occupants of the Haunted Mansion. There are many wonderful, and humorous, tributes to the lost animals. But did you know that this was not the first pet cemetery built at the Haunted Mansion? Did you know the original still exists today? If you did, have you been foolish enough to see it?

ABOVE: The well-known pet cemetery in front of the Haunted Mansion.

Disneyland built the first pet cemetery at the Haunted Mansion on the north side in the early 1980's. Just like out front, each pet was given its own epitaph on their grave marker. (EN: 60) It was so popular that Disneyland built one in the queue of the Haunted Mansion in 1993. The original is generally off limits to Guests, but if it's not too busy, and you ask the right Cast Member nicely, they may escort you back there for a quick look. (EN:58)

ABOVE: This is your first view of the secret pet cemetery as you are escorted past the gate onto the west side of the Haunted Mansion.

ABOVE: The original pet cemetery is between the Haunted Mansion and Splash Mountain. There is a small walkway between the Haunted Mansion and the Pet Cemetery. The crypts on the right are part of the ones Guests exit the Haunted Mansion from. The actual crypt you exit from is just out of the picture to the right.

LEFT AND BELOW: FROG - R.I.P. Bully, You didn't drink, You Didn't smoke, I just can't figure what made you croak.

RIGHT AND BELOW: SKUNK - In loving memory of our pet Stripey, You may be departed, but your presence will always linger on.

ABOVE LEFT AND ABOVE: CAT - In Memoriam Miss Kitty, After losing eight lives you still had no fear, you caught a snake in your ninth and that's why you are here.

BELOW AND RIGHT: DOG - Big Jake, Here lies my good dog Jake, chasing a toad down a well was his one mistake.

ABOVE: What is this in the center of the secret pet cemetery? Is it the tomb of the unknown pet? It is rumored that the plant atop this tombstone is often found knocked off in the morning. Are playful spooks at work here? (EN: 122)

BELOW: A closer look at the part of the Haunted Mansion crypts. The one that Guests exit from is behind the tree on the right.

RIGHT: The first room you encounter when entering the Haunted Mansion is the Foyer. There, the Ghost Host begins the narration of his tour. Take a look at the wallpaper. It has lilies, leaves, and is very ornate. Take a closer look. Did you notice the repeating pattern? It looks remarkably like a bat.

ABOVE: A closer look, with the bat figure highlighted.

ABOVE: If you've ever been unfortunate enough to be at Disneyland when the Haunted Mansion is closed, then you've seen this view. Take a closer look at the ornate gate, though. You will see the shapes of hearts and ship's steering wheels. This is a reference to one of the Haunted Mansion's early back stories. In this story, the Mansion was owned by Captain Gore, a notorious pirate. When his love, Prícilla, discovers his secret, she disappears under various suspicious circumstance. The captain was tormented by her demise and he committed suicide. (EN: 315)

ABOVE: After exiting the stretching room, most people are fascinated by the changing portraits and busts on the walls as they walk to board their Doom Buggies. Have you looked at the walls? There is some wonderful wood work, and if you look closely, you may find that there is a faces staring back at your.

BELOW: You are probably aware in the portrait gallery that there are chains guiding you towards the Doom Buggies. Did you look at the stanchions that are holding up the chains? Why they are just some friendly bats helping to guide you on your way...ha ha ha ha ha!

RIGHT: As you enter the attic, you become aware that a slow paced rendition of "Here Comes the Bride" is playing. As you round the corner towards the Black Widow Bride, you may notice towards the wall that there is a piano with nobody playing it. Or is there? Look at the back wall and you will see the shadow of the man playing the piano.

ABOVE (3) AND BELOW (2): You've probably noticed that as you travel around the attic, you see portraits of the Black Widow Bride with five different men. These are portraits of her with her five husbands. Have you watched the portraits closely? The heads of each of her Husbands disappear periodically. This of course is a subtle hint as to what the fate of each of her husbands was, or as she says, "I do...I did". Look near each portrait and you will also see a hat box. Are they there to give them a place to put their heads, like the infamous Hat Box Ghost? (EN: 321)

LEFT, BELOW, AND BOTTOM: Just past the piano player, we see the Constance Hatchaway (EN:y320), the Black Widow Bride herself. You've seen this, but did you look behind her and see her wedding cake? Maybe. But look closely and you will see that the Groom on the cake topper is, well, headless.

ABOVE: In the chapter on Tributes, I shared many of the hidden and not so hidden Un-Seen tributes to the people who contributed to the Park. Now you may be wondering, "are those names on the Christmas Naughty and Nice list a tribute?" Well, you'd be right. All of the names on the list are those of Disney Imagineers and others who worked on the Haunted Mansion Holiday overlay. (EN: 87)

QUIZ: Let's do another quiz. Can you name the other two Attractions that have tribute Naughty and Nice lists? (Answer EN: 243)

ABOVE AND BELOW: As part of the Haunted Mansion Holiday, the final scene with the Hitchhiking Ghosts is replaced with Oogie Boogie and his Holiday Tricks and Treats wheel. This fun saw, I mean wheel, has many great prizes. Look again at the wheel. Notice anything wrong with it? All of the prizes are placed so that they can be read by Guests. On a real wheel of fortune, they would all have their tops in the same direction.

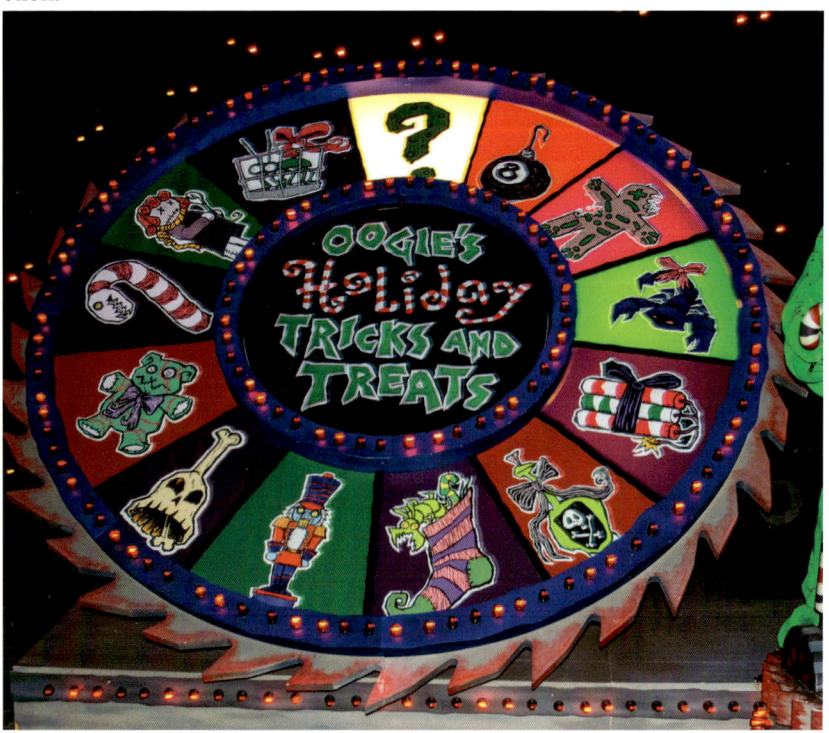

ABOVE: When the Haunted Mansion was being built, they used the face of Imagineer Leota Toombs for Madame Leota. The voice was provided by Eleanor Audley. Most would agree that they did a wonderful job combining these two in order to create the classic Madame Leota. This illusion is referred to by Imagineers as the "Leota Effect", a fitting tribute to Leota Toombs. (EN: 173)

BELOW: in 2001, Disneyland introduced a Christmas overlay based on Tim Burton's *The Nightmare Before Christmas*. They needed to re-do Madame Leota's scene, but sadly, Leota Toombs had passed away in 1991. Who could they get to replace her? Thankfully Leota's daughter Kim Irvine worked for Imagineering, and looks a lot like her mother. The new scene was shot with Kim and now the two share a place in Disney history.
(EN: 175 / 176)

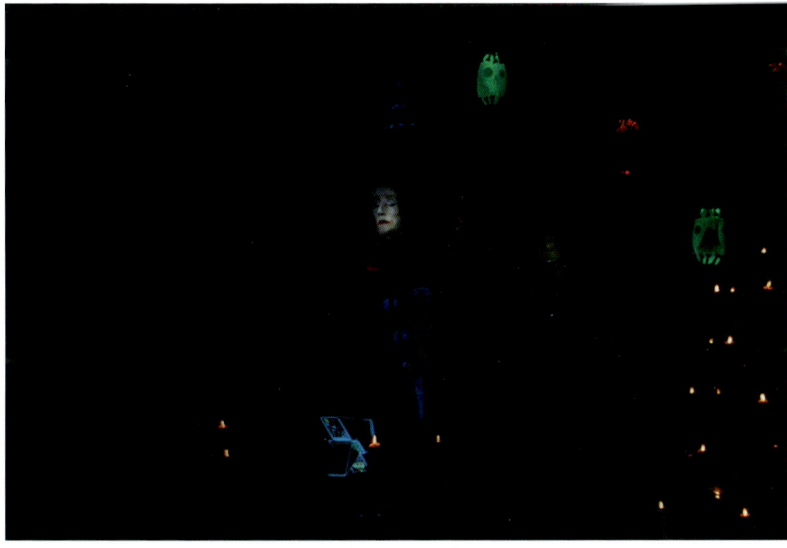

ABOVE: After you exit your Doom Buggy and go up the walkway, you will see this little character to your left. Her proper name is Ghostess, although she is commonly called Little Leota, with good reason. Her face and voice are those of Leota Toombs. (EN: 177)

LEFT AND BELOW: The clock inside the Haunted Mansion is famous for its 13 hours, devil-tail pendulum, and creepy hand shadow going across its face. Have you stopped to look at the clock out front of the Haunted Mansion? Take a closer look at the hour hand and you will find that it too has a creepy devil's tail.

ABOVE AND BELOW: The Indian Head Penny was made from 1859 to 1909. The date on the Penny above the entrance is completely legitimate. So why did the Imagineers pick 1901 as the date for their Indian Head Penny? That's an easy one. Walt Disney was born on December 5th, 1901. (EN: 76)

Have you noticed how wonderful the smells are at the Disneyland Candy Palace and the Gibson Girls Ice Cream Parlor? This is due to a special device known as a Smellitzer. This device is used to entice Guests with their wonderful aroma as they pass these stores on Main Street, U.S.A.. Smellitzers are also used in many attractions to give them their unique smells. (EN: 264)

NOTE: During the Christmas holiday season, Disneyland does several limited run candy cane batches. When they add the peppermint to the candy canes, the smell is wonderful.

This smell is not due to the Smellitzers. According to a guide in 2013, the peppermint is so concentrated, that the smell is actually escaping from the store. If you look at the candy makers, you can often see their eyes watering from the overwhelming smell.

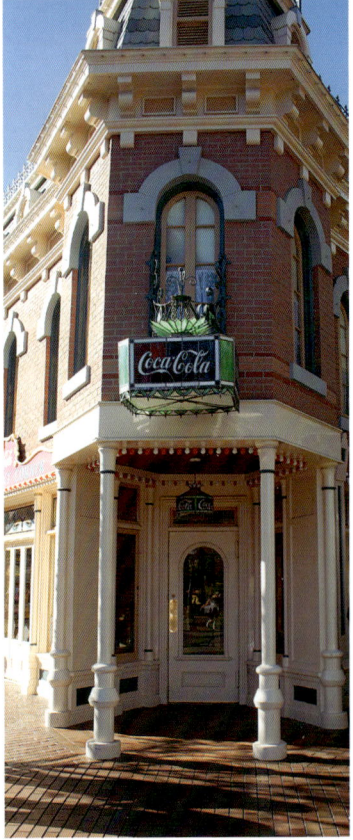

LEFT: Have you ever stopped to look at the flashing lights at Snack Corner (commonly known as Coke Corner)? Next time, look a little closer at the light bulb to the right of the entrance. When they installed the lights, they came up with an odd number. This meant that there would have to be two red or two white light bulbs next to each other. Rather than have this discrepancy, Walt Disney instructed the electricians to paint one light bulb half red and half white. The bulb was then installed so that it completed the alternating light pattern. (EN: 278)

ABOVE AND BELOW: As you walk under the Coca-Cola™ sign, look up and to your right and you will see the half-red and half-white light bulb.

QUIZ: How many light bulbs are there? (EN: 305)

As you stand under the flashing lights, look at the displays on either side of the door. Have you looked at the Coca-Cola™ bottle collection in the show cases?

There are bottles that date back to 1899, and from around the world. There are bottles from Japan and Israel.

There is even a bottle celebrating Coca-Cola's™ fiftieth anniversary, appropriately colored gold. You will even see a "prototype contour bottle" from the 1915's. A contour bottle is one that has that classic Coca-Cola™ shape that everyone is familiar with.

ABOVE AND RIGHT: Did you know that Walt Disney had a favorite booth at The Golden Horseshoe that he always used? Before Disneyland officially opened, Walt decided to hold a private party at the Park celebrating his and Lillian's 30th wedding anniversary. Although the party started on the Mark Twain, the main part of the party was held in The Golden Horseshoe. For this event, Walt choose to use the bottom right private box for his table (stage left). From that point on, this became the booth that Walt would use whenever he was at an event in The Golden Horseshoe. (EN:97)

Walt's brother Roy Disney preferred to sit at one of the center tables in front of the stage. (EN: 288)

ABOVE, LEFT, AND BELOW: Have you notice that above the first tunnel entrance on Big Thunder Mountain Railroad, there is a horseshoe hung with the opening up?

This is the correct way to hang a horseshoe so all the "luck" doesn't run out. This ensures a "safe" ride, or does it?

LEFT: As you enter the barn for the last lift (the big explosion scene), look up again. This horseshoe is hung the wrong way and all the "luck" is now gone. A sign of things to come.

THIS PAGE: While Rolly Crump was the Art Director of Disneyland, one of the problems he encountered was deterioration of the wooden set pieces, due to weather and their nightly cleaning by Cast Members. His solution was to replace these items with identical or similar fiberglass ones. The posts in front of the Frontierland Shooting Exposition are prime examples. They look just like real wood. If you touch them, you may still be fooled. Next time, tap on them and they will not make the familiar wooden knocking sound. (EN: 210)

LEFT AND RIGHT: Have you ever touched one of the "metal" light posts in New Orleans Square? You guessed it. They are not metal, but are made of fiberglass. Rolly Crump also had the light posts in New Orleans Square replaced with fiberglass ones that could better survive the elements. Many of the Main Street, U.S.A. light posts have been replaced too. Next time knock on a few and see if you can find them. (EN: 252)

LEFT: Look up at the front of the Opera House on Main Street and you will see several ornate golden figures. These too have been replaced with fiberglass. Don't try and knock on them though, as the Cast Members probably won't like you climbing on the building. (EN: 254)

ABOVE: Most things at Disneyland are built at a smaller scale and then forced perspective (DL) is used to make them look bigger. This is due to space and costs. The Columbia, however, is one of the few things that was actually built full-sized. When you go below deck and see the living quarters for the crew, that was the actual amount of space they had. The original 1787 Columbia was nicknamed "Gem of the Ocean". The Disneyland Columbia is nicknamed "Gem of the Kingdom. (EN: 232 / 245 / 249 / 273)

Another interesting fact is that there were no plans of the original Columbia to build Disneyland's version from, so plans of the H.M.S Bounty were used, as they were similar ships. (EN: 101 / 231)

RIGHT: Take a look at the rigging on the side. A nontraditional Hidden Mickey or just a happy coincidence? It's just standard rigging, but enjoy.

THIS PAGE: If you've ever been on the Jungle Cruise, then you obviously have seen, and heard, the revolvers used by the Skippers. These guns were on the boats on opening day to protect passengers from charging hippos, or at least those pesky ones in the trees. In 1999, the guns were removed from the attraction, but eventually returned in 2004.

What you may not know is that these are not prop guns. They are real, nickle plated, Smith and Wesson, .38 caliber revolvers. The chambers have been modified to not accept real ammunition. The guns are all registered with the FBI and are checked in and out each day. Two guns have been lost and reported stolen. After the second incident, a clip was added to secure the guns to the boats. The revolvers at Walt Disney World's Jungle Cruise have reportedly been replaced with prop guns.

During normal operation, the revolver is only fired one or two times. That is because the gun is also part of the Skipper's signal system for the attraction. If the Skipper fires 3 rounds, that signals the dock that the boat is having mechanical problems and cannot move. The foreman would then send help. If 4 shots are fired, it signals that the boat is having a medical or security problem. All boats will then proceed at their top safe speed to the dock and pass, allowing the distressed boat to come directly to the dock. If the Skipper fires 6 shots, that indicates the boat is derailed. No there is no 5 shot signal. (EN: 110)

QUIZ: There are 14 boats on the attraction. Can you name all of the boats? Bonus points: which ones were there on opening day? (Answer EN: 105)

As I explained on the previous page, guns have played a part of Disneyland since opening day; perhaps even more then you realized. On opening day, Davy Crockett (Fess Parker) and George Russel (Buddy Ebson) carried their trusty rifles when they appeared for the opening ceremonies. (EN: 233) There were even three shooting galleries at Disneyland over time, two of which used real .22 caliber rifles and ammunition. Some people consider the Davy Crockett Arcade as a fourth shooting gallery. It did have electronic shooting arcade games. They were each independent units and not setup in a traditional line. (EN: 235) In 1956, there was even a gun museum and store called American Rifle Exhibit and Frontier Gun Shop, located in Frontierland, where you could purchase replicas of the guns. (EN: 236)

The use of guns at Disneyland has changed with the times, but guns can still be found at the Park. In addition to the Jungle Cruise getting its guns back, The Laughing Stock Company show has actors who wear and shoot guns with blanks. Various attractions have guns as part of their theming. The Park even sells guns themed to various attractions. Buzz Lightyear Astro Blaster features a laser type gun as part of its operation. (EN: 307)

Disney takes guns very seriously, as displayed by the strict policy and monitoring of the Jungle Cruise's guns. In addition, they are very conscious and thoughtful of when and how guns are displayed in their shows and attractions. Whether realistic, futuristic, or fantasy, safe gun practices, and especially Guests' safety are paramount to Disney.

LEFT: The Skippers are not the only ones with guns on the Jungle Cruise. Watch out for this ape. He doesn't look like he has attended a gun safety class.

RIGHT: In the old west, guns were a necessity, especially for cavalry soldiers, even when in their fort. Just after entering Frontierland from the Hub, look behind the walls on the left side and you might see these rifles all lined up. You'll also see boxes of ammo along the walkway of the parapets.

QUIZ: Can you name the three shooting galleries and which used real ammunition? (Answers EN: 224)

208

If you turn to your right after entering the fort, you will see this cannon. It is ready to defend the fort. Well, maybe not. This cannon adds wonderful theming to the area, but has been made safe. The cannon balls are all attached to each other and the barrel is plugged.

RIGHT: Take a look at the little lean-to on the Tom Sawyer rafts. There you can find a musket and sword.

BELOW: And be careful where you sit, because you may be sitting on a barrel of Dynamite.

LEFT: In Buzz Lightyear Astro Blasters, Guests use their futuristic blaster to score points and save the galaxy.

In the first edition of my book series, I talked about the rumor that one of the pirates was reportedly a caricature of Walt Disney and how I learned that this was not true. I also learned during an interview that no individual pirate was based on any one singular person, except one. In the jail scene, one of the prisoners was based on one of the janitors at WED. During a subsequent interview, I learned that it was the pirate whistling for the dog. All other pirates, and characters in the Haunted Mansion, are a conglomeration of features from multiple peoples. (EN: 73 / 74)

ABOVE: One of the most iconic scenes from Pirates of the Caribbean, the three pirates trying to get a key from the dog.

RIGHT: A close-up of the only pirate reportedly based on a single person.

LEFT AND BELOW: Have you ever noticed these little guys in front of Pirates of the Caribbean? That's exactly the question my friend Chris asked me one day while we were standing in line. He told me that these "acorns" or "pineapples" were all over Disneyland. I was intrigued. I started looking and found that they could indeed be found all over the Park. I began taking pictures of them as I found them, and started researching to find what they were exactly. At first, my research indicated that they represented "pineapples" and that they were an "old", universal symbol for greetings or welcome. This would make sense for Walt Disney and the Imagineers to include such a object in the Park. Further research showed that this was actually a "new" interpretation.

They are called "finial". These ornate decorations can be placed on poles, bed posts, light stands, and flag poles. Finials are also used on the highest point of a roofs, domes, or any high points of a structure. They can also be ornamentation at the end of a pull chain for a light or fan. Finials can consist of pineapples, acorns, or any other decorative feature. They are strictly for decoration. As you wander around Disneyland, you will find several examples of finials. They are used on walls, lights, store displays, queues, and even fountains. Here are a few more finials I found around the Park. (EN: 77)

LEFT AND BELOW: These finial can be found on one of the entrance bridges to Fantasy Faire. This is the bridge that leads from the Hub to Fantasy Faire. Note these are still classic pineapples.

LEFT AND RIGHT: These can be found on the stone stair case leading Guests upstairs on Splash Mountain. They are acorns.

LEFT, RIGHT, AND BELOW: In front of it's a small world and along the promenade, you can find two different styles of finials used as area lights. They are both acorn or heart shaped, but one sits on top of the light post and the other hangs down from the light post.

213

LEFT: This finial looks like some sort of closed fruit. It can be seen on the blue fencing around the New Orleans Square waterfront.

LEFT: This egg shaped finial can be found on Main Street, U.S.A. in front of the Emporium.

RIGHT: This one has a pole coming out of the top of it for the Fire Engine loading zone sign. It can be found in front of City Hall.

LEFT: You can find this finial in front of Chip & Dale's Treehouse, in Toontown. It really is an acorn.

RIGHT: This artichoke finial can be seen hanging from the eaves of Mr. Toad's Wild Ride.

LEFT: Even store displays get into the act. This display can be found at Castle Brothers clothing store on Main Street, U.S.A.. The part of the rake that hold the hangers uses acorn finials for stops.

ABOVE: The railing for the queues in the Market House Starbucks™ has finials that look like pine cones.

RIGHT: Close-up.

BELOW: The fountain in the Magnolia Park (EN: 306), located between Haunted Mansion and the French Market Restaurant, has an interesting finial on

top of it. It looks like a well weathered pineapple. Next time you are at the Park, see how many finials you can find.

BELOW: Close-up.

ABOVE: As we all know, the entrance to the sacred Indian elephant bathing pool is guarded by Ganesh. He has a wonderful smile and looks like a really fun elephant.

BELOW: Look closer. You will see that he is using a snake as a belt. There are many versions of the story of how Ganesh got his snake belt. The basic story goes that he was celebrating and feasting. He became very full so he decided to go for a ride on his rat or shrew. His mount was startled by a snake and he fell off, breaking his stomach open. All his food was coming out. He quickly stuffed the feast back in and closed his stomach. Genesh grabbed the snake and used it as a belt to hold his food in. (EN: 237 /238)

Almost everyone who has been to Disneyland has seen the Horse-Drawn Street Cars travel up and down Main Street. On opening day, there were several different types of horse drawn vehicles on Main Street. In addition, there were pack mules, conestoga wagons, and stage coaches in Frontierland. Main Street represents the turn-of-the-century in the early 1900's. The automobile, or horseless carriage, was just coming out. This meant there were still a lot of horses in use, so there would have to be places for people to hitch them. If you look up and down Main Street and in Frontierland, you will see several hitching posts. You can even find a couple in New Orleans Square.

LEFT: The most prevalent hitching post in Disneyland is the horse head style. This one can be seen in front of the Main Street Opera House, which is the home of The Disneyland Story Presenting Great Moments with Mr. Lincoln.

BELOW RIGHT: These two can be seen in front of the Disney Showcase.

BELOW MIDDLE: A straight on view of a horse head hitching post.

BELOW LEFT: This wooden post is another one of those items that makes you wonder. It can be seen to the left of the former Wizard of Bras store (see more on this store on page 40).

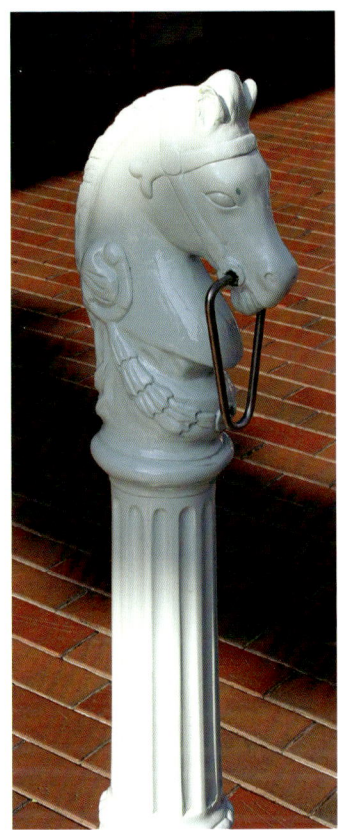

ABOVE: A hitching post in front of Cafe Orleans restaurant in New Orleans Square.

LEFT: A closer side view of one of the horse head hitching posts. You can see this one in front of the Emporium.

BELOW: A true wild west hitching post, or rail, in front of the Frontierland Shooting Exposition.

As you enter Frontierland through the fort's gates, have you noticed the flags that line the tops of the stockade?

LEFT: The 13 flags were carried by American troops at various times during the Revolutionary War. This sign can be found on the right gate and explains the significance of the various Continental flags.

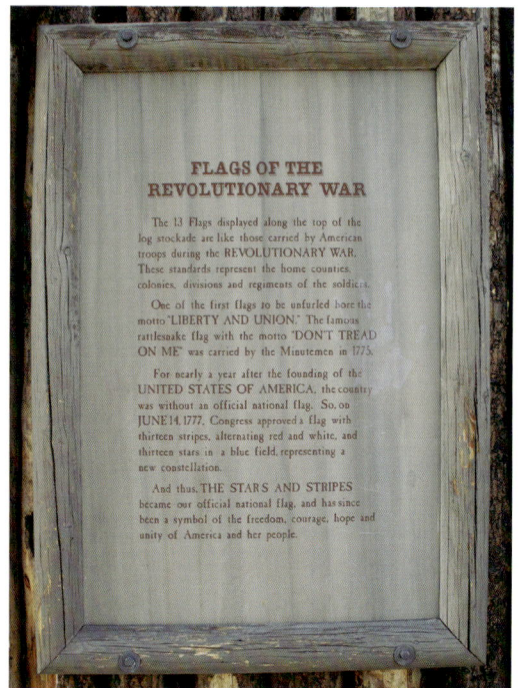

BELOW: These flags can be seen on the stockade to the left of the Frontierland gates. The first flag is the Taunton or "Liberty and Union" flag of the Sons of Liberty. This flag was used at their meetings. (EN: 256)

RIGHT: One of the best known of these Continental flags is the Gadsden Flag. This famous flag is yellow with a rattlesnake and immortal words "Don't Tread on Me". (EN: 255)

BELOW: Be sure to check out more flags on the right side of the gates.

ABOVE: When the trees and other plants are in full bloom, it is often easier to view the flags from inside of the fort.

BELOW: As you continue into Frontierland and approach the Sailing Ship Columbia and Mark Twain Riverboat dock, this is your normal view. Have you ever stopped to look at the left and right wings of the dock area? There are more flags here. People often presume that they are just a row of current American flags. They are so much more than that. The eight flags represented served important roles in United States history. They start with the Cabot Flag from the Mayflower and end with our Old Glory. The following two pages shows each of the flags. Let's take a closer look.

WASTE PLEASE

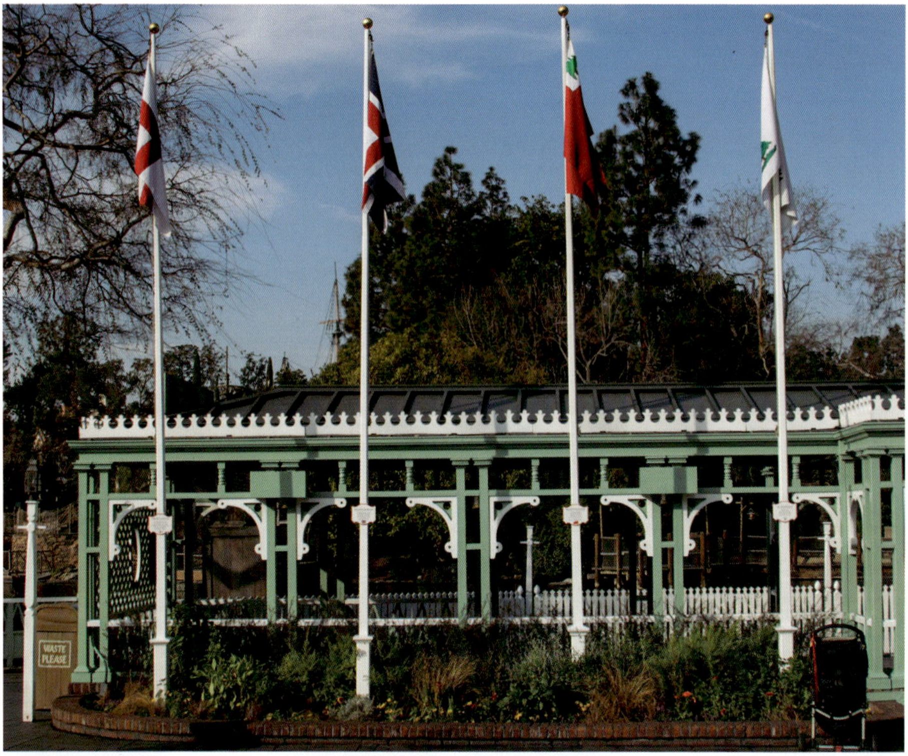

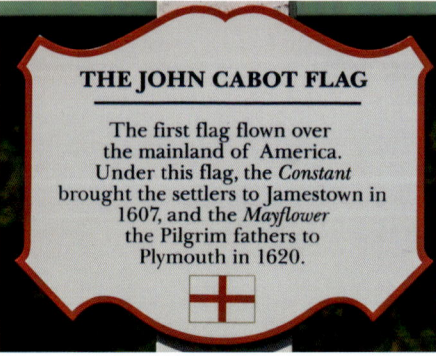

THE JOHN CABOT FLAG
The first flag flown over the mainland of America. Under this flag, the *Constant* brought the settlers to Jamestown in 1607, and the *Mayflower* the Pilgrim fathers to Plymouth in 1620.

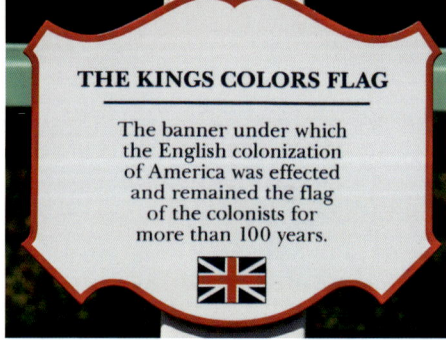

THE KINGS COLORS FLAG
The banner under which the English colonization of America was effected and remained the flag of the colonists for more than 100 years.

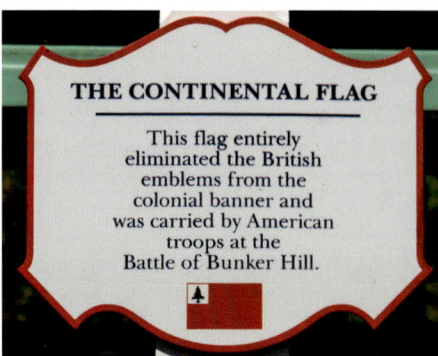

THE CONTINENTAL FLAG
This flag entirely eliminated the British emblems from the colonial banner and was carried by American troops at the Battle of Bunker Hill.

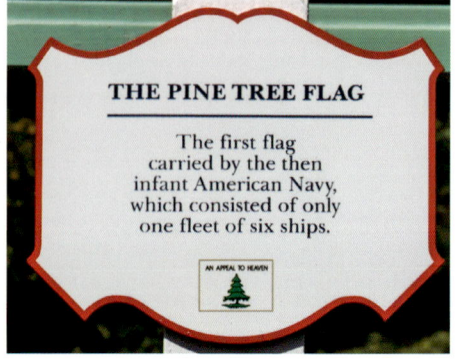

THE PINE TREE FLAG
The first flag carried by the then infant American Navy, which consisted of only one fleet of six ships.
AN APPEAL TO HEAVEN

THE GRAND UNION FLAG

This flag marks the beginning of our national existence and was raised at Cambridge by General Washington in 1776.

THE BETSY ROSS FLAG
13 Stars and 13 Stripes

The first American flag formally adopted by the Continental Congress in 1777. The stars symbolize the new constellation of states rising in the west. The stripes represent the number of United Colonies.

THE STAR SPANGLED BANNER
15 Stars and 15 Stripes

This flag inspired Francis Scott Key to write the words of our national anthem during the British attack on Fort McHenry in 1814.

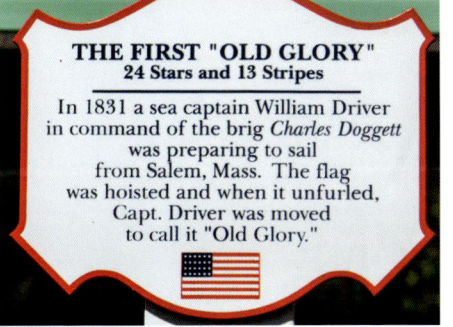

THE FIRST "OLD GLORY"
24 Stars and 13 Stripes

In 1831 a sea captain William Driver in command of the brig *Charles Doggett* was preparing to sail from Salem, Mass. The flag was hoisted and when it unfurled, Capt. Driver was moved to call it "Old Glory."

Over time, there have been several fences around the Submarine Lagoon and Autopia. Did you know you can see a time capsule of three of the fences all in the same place? They are called The Three Fences. If you follow the fence around the lagoon from the submarines queue, towards the Matterhorn, keep going until you walk under the Monorail Track. (EN: 120)

ABOVE: Here you will see where three different fences all meet together.

RIGHT: The blueish-green fence is the current fence around the lagoon. The black fence is what was left after Fantasyland Autopia was removed. The white fence is all that remains of the original Submarine Lagoon fence from its opening day.

LEFT: Looking straight down on where the three fences meet. The original white and replacement Autopia black fences are attached to each other. The current Submarine Lagoon fence is free standing.

QUIZ: Each of the submarines has a name. Can you name them all? Bonus, they have actually had three sets of names. Can you give the years and the names? (Answer EN: 298)

THIS PAGE: If you stop and look at the supports for the retired People Mover, you will notice that there is something organic about them. That is because they are based on the look of trees. One of the themes of Tomorrowland was food. All of the plants used in Tomorrowland are edible. (EN: 279) In keeping with this theme, and to make the supports more comfortable and appealing to the Guests, Disney Imagineer John Hench and Disney Sculptor Mitsu made the supports to resemble trees. This gives them a beautiful and elegant look and feel.
(EN: 108)

LEFT: When the sun goes down, the beauty of these structures continues with the expert placement of lighting and color by Disney Imagineers.

ABOVE: Winner's Circle was formerly known as The Mod Hatter and The Hatmosphere.

RIGHT: The bottom level of the former People Mover / Rocket Jets was the west coast Radio Disney booth from 1999 - 2002. The space remained closed until 2006. (EN: 160 / 274)

LEFT: The space reopened as Tomorrowlanding and now can service all of your hat needs.

Have you ever noticed that there are two stores with the same name at Disneyland? The marquee for the hat store on Main Street says The Mad Hatter and the one in Fantasyland says Mad Hatter. Officially, they are known as The Mad Hatter on Main Street U.S.A. and The Mad Hatter in Fantasyland. (EN: 124)

There use to be three stores named Mad Hatter. The third Mad Hatter was originally located about where The Star Trader is located today. During the 1966/1967 re-furb, it was moved next to the entrance to Autopia. It was renamed The Mod Hatter in order to make the name more contemporary. Later, it was again renamed to The Hatmosphere to better fit in with the Tomorrowland theme. In 2006, the Winner's Circle took over this space. (EN: 123 / 129)

Don't worry though, your hat needs can still be fulfilled. After replacing the Hatmosphere, the Radio Disney booth located under the Observatron was replaced with a store called Tomorrow Landing. The store featured merchandise related to the various Tomorrowland attractions. Eventually, it became a generic hat store. (EN: 125 / 126)

ABOVE: The Mad Hatter in Fantasyland.

LEFT: The Mad Hatter on Main Street USA.

BELOW: Take a look at the Mad Hatter's hat band. The 10/6 isn't a hat size or the Mad Hatter being crazy. It's actually part of the old British monetary system of pounds, shillings, and pennies (or pence). It means the hat cost 10 shillings, 6 pence. (EN: 128)

ABOVE: As you enter the Enchanted Chamber, look to your left. Notice the hole in the wall sitting on the pillar? It's not really obvious if you're not looking for it. It appears to be a storm drain and it is pointed right at the door. "That's strange". If it is not a storm drain, what is it? Seems like a very strange place for a drain.
(EN: 261)

RIGHT: A closer look at this mysterious hole.

BELOW LEFT AND RIGHT: So, you may be asking, this is just a one time thing, right? Well, maybe not. Next time you walk by one of my favorite restaurants in the Park, Carnation Café, look up. About three quarters of the way up, just under the eves and directly over the left door, what do you see? Yep, there is another drain.

BELOW LEFT, MIDDLE, AND RIGHT: Look on the wall between the Adventureland Bazaar door and Bengal Barbecue. There you will see not one, but two, drains.

I actually have been to Disneyland many times when it is raining. I have never seen water coming out of any of these drains.

229

The next time you are on Peter Pan's Flight, take a look at the clothes that the characters are wearing. Notice anything? Only Wendy is wearing real cloth clothes. (EN: 127)

LEFT: In this scene, Captain Hook and Smee are making Wendy walk the plank. Don't worry, the nice nightgown won't be ruined by the sea. Peter Pan is fighting Captain Hook to save the day.

BELOW: In the final scene, Peter Pan is steering the ship with Michael and John to his right and Wendy to his left. Look at all their clothes. She is the only one with real cloth clothes on.

How about a couple of head scratchers? Here are a few more "that's strange" pictures.

ABOVE: In the final scene of The Many Adventures of Winnie the Pooh, our favorite bear can be seen celebrating his good fortune with his friends. There are five slices of cake that have been cut out. Look at the un-cut cake. It looks like only a two or three pieces were removed. Where did all of that cake come from? (EN: 260)

LEFT: A closer look at the cake shows that at most, three slices have been removed.

BELOW: Here are three slices of cake sitting on the left end of the table.

LEFT: But here are two more slices of cake sitting on the right side of the table. Where did they come from? Was there another cake? We may never know.

ABOVE AND BELOW: As you walk up to the entrance of Roger Rabbit's Car Toon Spin, look to you left and you will notice the attraction has a second story balcony. This is not unusual, as many attraction facades have second story balconies. However, this one was originally going to serve a purpose. During the planning of Roger Rabbit's Car Toon Spin, it was originally planned to be a two story attraction. After going upstairs, the cab at some point would burst out of the building, onto this balcony, and then re-enter the building before going back down stairs. It would have been similar to how Alice in Wonderland goes outside, only much more dynamic. It was decided to make the attraction single story for technical reasons, but the balcony was left on the facade.
(EN: 188 / 189 / 190)

ABOUT THE AUTHOR

ABOVE: The author relaxing on the porch of the former Hollywood Maxwell's Company: Intimate Apparel, Brassieres, Torsolettes. Also known as The Wizard of Bras.

Russell was born and raised on the Central California Coast. Living only three-and-a-half hours from Disneyland, Russell was fortunate enough to get to visit the Park several times a year while growing up. From 1968 to 1980, he visited Disneyland over thirty-six times. After that, he only visited Disneyland once a year or so until the birth of his only child. In 1991, Russell met his future wife who is also a big fan of Disneyland. They visited Disneyland twice before getting married in 1993. For their honeymoon, they went to Walt Disney World. It was the first trip for both of them. In 1995 they moved to Sacramento. They were then seven hours from Disneyland, making trips only once every few years. In 2000 they had their one and only child. Russell and his wife, wanting their child to share in the same joys of going to Disneyland as they had as children, starting taking her at age three. That year, they took two trips and quickly bought annual passes and a stone marker in the Esplanade. They also discovered that to make the travel easier, they would go for one week trips rather than more frequent, shorter trips. This lead to their twice-a-year trip schedule. In 2008, they all went to Walt Disney World for Russ and his wife's fifteenth wedding anniversary.

They are also fortunate enough to have several friends who are Disney fans. They enjoy taking trips with friends and family, as well as trips by themselves. They have visited The Walt Disney Family Museum in San Francisco and The Walt Disney Studios in Burbank. They also enjoy participating in Disneyland events such as the Disneyland Half Marathons (Disneyland, Star Wars, and Tinker Bell), D23 Expo and other D23 events, Mickey's Very Merry Christmas Party (Walt Disney World), Mickey's Not So Scary Halloween Party (Disneyland), Be Our Guest Dinner, and the Pacific Northwest Mouse Meet. They are Disneyland Annual Pass Holders, Disney Vacation Club (DVC) members, Walt Disney Family Museum members, Disney Stock Holders, and D23 members.

Follow me on Facebook and Twitter for more information about future books in the series and other great Disney related information. Watch for *Seen, Un-Seen Disneyland: California Adventure Edition*.

Facebook

http://www.facebook.com/seenunseendisneyland

Twitter

http://www.twitter.com/seenunseend

The "Interwebs"

http://www.sudbooks.com

This isn't the end of the story. Watch for more books in the Seen, Un-Seen Series.

END NOTES (EN)

#1 Pat Williams with Jim Denney, How to Be Like Walt: Capturing the Disney Magic Every Day of Your Life (Deerfield: Health Communications, Inc., 2004), p. 154.

#2 Pat Williams with Jim Denney, How to Be Like Walt: Capturing the Disney Magic Every Day of Your Life (Deerfield: Health Communications, Inc., 2004), p. 174.

#3 Bob Thomas, Walt Disney: An American Original (New York: Disney Editions, 1976, 1994), p. 288.

Walt Disney Famous Quotes (Lake Buena Vista: The Walt Disney Company, 1994), p. 36.

#4 Bob Thomas, Walt Disney: An American Original (New York: Disney Editions, 1976, 1994), p. 289.

#5 Bob Thomas, Walt Disney: An American Original (New York: Disney Editions, 1976, 1994), p. 266.

#6 Bob Thomas, Walt Disney: An American Original (New York: Disney Editions, 1976, 1994), p. 264.

#7 Bob Thomas, Walt Disney: An American Original (New York: Disney Editions, 1976, 1994), p. 262.

#8 Amy Boothe Green and Howard E. Green, Remembering Walt: Favorite Memories of walt Disney (New York: Disney Editions, 1999), p. 163.

#9 Amy Boothe Green and Howard E. Green, Remembering Walt: Favorite Memories of walt Disney (New York: Disney Editions, 1999), p. 67.

#10 Amy Boothe Green and Howard E. Green, Remembering Walt: Favorite Memories of Walt Disney (New York: Disney Editions, 1999), p. 152.

#11 Amy Boothe Green and Howard E. Green, Remembering Walt: Favorite Memories of walt Disney (New York: Disney Editions, 1999), p. 156.

#12 Amy Boothe Green and Howard E. Green, Remembering Walt: Favorite Memories of walt Disney (New York: Disney Editions, 1999), p. 158.

#13 Randy Bright, Disneyland Inside story (New York: Harry N. Abrams, Inc., 1987), p. 187.

#14 Michael Broggie, Walt Disney's Railroad Story: The Small-Scale Fascination That Led to a Full-Scale Kingdom (Pasadena: Pentrex Media Group, 1997), p. 245.

#15 Michael Broggie, Walt Disney's Railroad Story: The Small-Scale Fascination That Led to a Full-Scale Kingdom (Pasadena: Pentrex Media Group, 1997), p. 248.

#16 Michael Broggie, Walt Disney's Railroad Story: The Small-Scale Fascination That Led to a Full-Scale Kingdom (Pasadena: Pentrex Media Group, 1997), p. 279.

#17 Michael Broggie, Walt Disney's Railroad Story: The Small-Scale Fascination That Led to a Full-Scale Kingdom (Pasadena: Pentrex Media Group, 1997), p. 29.

#18 Steve DeGaetano, Welcome aboard the Disneyland Railroad!: The Complete Disneyland railroad Reference Guide (Winnetka: Steam Passeges Publications, 2004), p. 40.

#19 Steve DeGaetano, Welcome aboard the Disneyland Railroad!: The Complete Disneyland railroad Reference Guide (Winnetka: Steam Passeges Publications, 2004), p. 48.

#20 Michael Broggie, Walt Disney's Railroad Story: The Small-Scale Fascination That Led to a Full-Scale Kingdom (Pasadena: Pentrex Media Group, 1997), p. 220.

#21 Steve DeGaetano, Welcome aboard the Disneyland Railroad!: The Complete Disneyland railroad Reference Guide (Winnetka: Steam Passages Publications, 2004), p. 223.

#22 wikipedia.com, Disneyland railroad, http://en.wikipedia.org/wiki/Disneyland_Railroad (8/14/2012).

#23 Michael Broggie, Walt Disney's Railroad Story: The Small-Scale Fascination That Led to a Full-Scale Kingdom (Pasadena: Pentrex Media Group, 1997), pp. 61 - 91.

Steve DeGaetano, Welcome aboard the Disneyland Railroad!: The Complete Disneyland railroad Reference Guide (Winnetka: Steam Passeges Publications, 2004), p. 30.

Michael Broggie, Email (10/9/2014).

#24 The name of the road is Schumacher Road, based on a photograph I took of a road sign posted on it. I also found a reference that called it Service Road. It is a small portion of a larger road that generally circles just inside the berm called Berm Road. In my research to identify who Schumacher Road was named for, I found two Schumachers who worked for The Walt Disney Company. In Van France's book, he identifies Fred Schumacher as the one who the road is named after. Fred worked for Walt Disney during the constructions of the park and was instrumental in getting those all too important early sponsors. He later became the, General Services Director, Park Operating Committee: 11/58 - 8/8/59. This position eventually became known as The Disneyland Resort President. Jack Lindquist was the first to actually hold that title. The small piece of the road that goes from the train tracks to the gate by its a small world is un-officially called "small world step off".

Russell Flores, Photograph of road sign identifying the road as Schumacher Road.

Van Arsdale France, Window On Main Street: 35 Years of Creating Happiness at Disneyland Park (Nashua, NH: Laughter Publications, Inc., 1991), p. 12.

Ken Pellman, Co-Host The Sweep Spot Podcast, identified the un-official working name of the small portion of road, email interview, (6/15/2014).

Steve DeGaetano, Welcome aboard the Disneyland Railroad!: The Complete Disneyland railroad Reference Guide (Winnetka: Steam Passeges Publications, 2004), p. 219.

Disney History Institute, The 1939 World's Fair and Disneyland, http://www.disneyhistoryinstitute.com/2012_10_01_archive.html (8/8/2012).

B Guthrie Photos, CA -- Anaheim -- Disneyland -- Notes:, http://www.bguthriephotos.com/graphlib.nsf/keys/1969_CA_Disneyland?OpenDocument&Desc Full (6/15/2014).

Disneyland Nomenclature: Building a Disneyland Encyclopedia, day by day, 4,542 Terms (and Not Done Yet), http://disneylandcompendium.blogspot.com/2012/12/4542-terms-and-not-done-yet.html, (12/17/2012).

#25 www.doombuggies.com, Brigham Young's Hearse?, http://www.doombuggies.com/secrets_facade.php (7/6/2014).

#26 www.holyfetch.com, The Hearse in front of the Haunted Mansion at Disneyland carried Brigham Young, http://www.holyfetch.com/Mormons_in_entertainment/disney_hearse.html (7/6/2014).

#27 Lynn Arave, Disney Hearse has no link to Brigham Young, http://www.deseretnews.com/article/827116/Disney-hearse-has-no-link-to-Brigham-Young.html?pg=all (2/23/2001).

#28 Chris Strodder, The Disneyland Encyclopedia: The UNOfficial, UNAuthorized, and UNPrecedented History of Every Land, Attraction, Restaurant, Shop, and Event in the Original Magic Kingdom: Updated Second Edition (Santa Monica: Santa Monica Press LLC., 2012), p. 207.

#29 "dan", The Haunted Mansion Hearse and Brigham Young, http://www.dadlogic.net/2012/10/19/the-haunted-mansion-hearse-and-brigham-young/ (10/19/2012).

#30 On April 21, 2013, I was fortunate enough to be able to ride on the Lille Belle before they discontinue public rides. During the tour, the cast member shared the history of the jacket.

#31 Disneyland Report, Hidden Gems: Real Bones on Pirates of the Caribbean, http://disneylandreport.blogspot.com/2013/05/hidden-gems-real-bones-on-pirates-of.html (5/15/2013).

#32 Tony Baxter, I spoke with Tony Baxter about Thunder Mountain (6/28/2014).

#33 Werner Weiss, The Wizard of Bras At Hollywood-Maxwell's Intimate Apparel Shop, http://www.yesterland.com/wizard.html (5/29/2008).

#34 Sam Gennawey, A front porch fit for the Wizard of Bras, http://micechat.com/16063-disneyland-wizard-of-bras/ (11/15/2012).

#35 Werner Weiss, Tobacco Shop, http://www.yesterland.com/tobaccoshop.html (3/19/2014).

#36 The location of the three current smoking locations at Disneyland as of 1/1/2015 are as follows:
    1. Under the Monorail tracks where the old Fantasyland Autopia cars use to load. This is on the east side of the Fantasyland walkway, between the submarine ride and the Edelweiss Snack shack.
    2. The former Mike Fink loading docks. This area is located on the Rivers of America between the Tom Sawyer Rafts and Fowler's Harbor. (see page 143zzz)
    3. Until December of 2014, the third location for smoking was on the back side of Big Thunder Mountain, on Big Thunder trail, between the bridge and the entrance to the Big Thunder Ranch. When the Fantasmic Fast Pass station was created, the smoking area was moved further up the trail just before the entrance to Fantasyland.

#37 Weiss, Werner, Tobacco Shop, http://www.yesterland.com/tobaccoshop.html (3/19/2014).

#38 Dave DeCaro, July 18, 1955 Extravaganza, Pt. 1, http://davelandblog.blogspot.com/2012/07/july-18-1955-extravaganza-pt-1.html (7/19/2012).

Jewel (Edited by Adrienne Krock), Sleeping Beauty Castle, http://www.mouseplanet.com/magicyears/my122200.htm (7/13/2014).

#39 Mr. Toad's Wild Ride is the only attraction that has the word "Ride" actually in its name. Don't worry if you thought there were more. We'll look at this idea more in a later chapter.

#40 Jeff Baham, An Unofficial Hostory of Dinsey's Haunted Mansion (USA: DoomBuggies.com, 2010), p. 40.

#41 Michael Broggie, Walt Disney's Railroad Story: The Small-Scale Fascination That Led to a Full-Scale Kingdom (Pasadena: Pentrex Media Group, 1997), pp. 214 / 268.

#42 Michael Broggie, Walt Disney's Railroad Story: The Small-Scale Fascination That Led to a Full-Scale Kingdom (Pasadena: Pentrex Media Group, 1997), p. 233.

#43 Michael Broggie, Walt Disney's Railroad Story: The Small-Scale Fascination That Led to a Full-Scale Kingdom (Pasadena: Pentrex Media Group, 1997), p. 235.

#44 Justin Scarred, Five Weird Things in Fantasyland - Disneyland, https://www.youtube.com/watch?v=2HcXfCPAg0M&feature=em-subs_digest (8/17/2014).

#45 Dave Smith, Disney A to Z: The Updated Official Encyclopedia (New York: Hyperion, 1996/1998), p. 66.

#46 J. B. Kaufman, South of the Border with Disney: Walt Disney and the Good Neighbor Program, 1941 - 1948 (New York: Disney Editions, 2009), p. 28.

#47 Mary Blair, International Movie Database (IMBb), http://www.imdb.com/name/nm0086304/?ref_=fn_al_nm_1 (8/24/2014).

#48 Rolly Crump, It's Kind Of a Cute Story (U.S.A: Bamboo Forest Publishing, 2012), p. 70.

#49 Rolly Crump, former Imagineer, email interview (August 28, 2014).

#50 Kevin Yee, Walt Disney World Hidden History (Orlando: Ultimate Orlando Press, 2010), p. 56.

#51 The Sweep Spot Podcast, Show #69 Interview with Sam Gennawey (10/6/2012), www.thesweepspot.com.

#52 Rolly Crump, It's Kind Of a Cute Story (U.S.A: Bamboo Forest Publishibg, 2012), p. 69.

#53 Rolly Crump, It's Kind Of a Cute Story (U.S.A: Bamboo Forest Publishibg, 2012), p. 75.

#54 The DisGeek Podcast, Show #77 Big Thunder Strikes back, www.disgeek.com (3/23/2014).

#55 Chris Strodder, The Disneyland Encyclopedia: The UNOfficial, UNAuthorized, and UNPrecedented History of Every Land, Attraction, Restaurant, Shop, and Event in the Original Magic Kingdom Updated Second Edition (Santa Monica: Santa Monica Press LLC., 2012), p. 178.

#56 Chris Strodder, The Disneyland Encyclopedia: The UNOfficial, UNAuthorized, and UNPrecedented History of Every Land, Attraction, Restaurant, Shop, and Event in the Original Magic Kingdom Updated Second Edition (Santa Monica: Santa Monica Press LLC., 2012), p. 81.

#57 Chris Strodder, The Disneyland Encyclopedia: The UNOfficial, UNAuthorized, and UNPrecedented History of Every Land, Attraction, Restaurant, Shop, and Event in the Original Magic Kingdom Updated Second Edition (Santa Monica: Santa Monica Press LLC., 2012), pp. 280/283/87/141/351/ 239/442/208.

#58 Secrets of the Haunted Mansion: The Facade and Queue Areas, In memorium: Remembering man's best friends, http://www.doombuggies.com/secrets_queue.php (9/6/2014).

duchessofdisneyland, Haunted Mansion Pet Cemetery, http://duchessofdisneyland.com/2014/04/10/haunted-mansion-pet-cemetery/ (April 10, 2014).

#59   1. Merlin's Magic Shop - July 17,1955 (opening day) to January 16, 1983
2. Mickey's Christmas Chalet - May 25, 1983 to May 17, 1987
3. Briar Rose Cottage - May 29, 1987 to July 15, 1991
4. Disney Villians - July 16, 1991 to June 21, 1996
5. Quasimododo's Attic / Sanctuary of Quasimodo
   June 21, 1996 to February 1997
6. Knight Shop - August 16, 1997 to October 3, 1998
7. Villians Lair - October 3, 1998 to July 1, 2004
8. Heraldry Shoppe - The Heraldry Shoppe opend in 1995, inside the Castle, it moved to this location in 2004.
Note: This is not a continuos time line due to construction and at times, the location was closed and unused.

Chris Strodder, The Disneyland Encyclopedia: The UNOfficial, UNAuthorized, and UNPrecedented History of Every Land, Attraction, Restaurant, Shop, and Event in the Original Magic Kingdom Updated Second Edition (Santa Monica: Santa Monica Press LLC., 2012), p. 280/283/87/141/351/ 239/442/208.

#60 The Pet Cemeteries, http://longforgottenhauntedmansion.blogspot.com/2010/07/pet-cemeteries.html (July 19, 2010).

#61 Chris Strodder, The Disneyland Encyclopedia: The UNOfficial, UNAuthorized, and UNPrecedented History of Every Land, Attraction, Restaurant, Shop, and Event in the Original Magic Kingdom Updated Second Edition (Santa Monica: Santa Monica Press LLC., 2012), p. 116-117.

#62 Paul Barrie, Window to the Magic Podcast, email interview (September 9, 2014).

#63 Paul Barrie, Country Bear Jamboree, http://doneinthedark.com/ (September 9, 2014).

The Disney Wiki, Country Bear Jamboree, http://disney.wikia.com/wiki/Country_Bear_Jamboree (September 8, 2014).

Country Bear Jamboree Facebook page, https://www.facebook.com/groups/1442124642668151/ (September 10, 2014).

Matthew Walker, Country Bears Permanent hibernation, http://www.startedbyamouse.com/happenings/CBJ01.shtml (September 10, 2014).

allears.net, Country Bear Jamboree - Part Two, http://land.allears.net/blogs/jackspence/walt_disney_world/theme_parks/magic_kingdom/frontierland/country_bear_jamboree/ (October 28, 2010).

laughingplace.com, Disneyland to close the Country Bears on Sep 9, http://www.laughingplace.com/News-ID10007910.asp (August 23, 2001).

disneyfans.com, At The Magic Kingdom Only:The Country Bear Jamboree, http://www.disneyfans.com/dlvstmk/tmkonly/tmk_countrybears.shtml (September 10, 2014).

#64 Chris Strodder, The Disneyland Encyclopedia: The UNOfficial, UNAuthorized, and UNPrecedented History of Every Land, Attraction, Restaurant, Shop, and Event in the Original Magic Kingdom Updated Second Edition (Santa Monica: Santa Monica Press LLC., 2012), p. 219.

#65 Big Thunder Mountain Railroad is the proper title for this attraction. However, it is referred to as the "wildest ride in the wilderness". This making it the only other attraction where it is proper to refer to it as a ride too.

#66 Chris Strodder, The Disneyland Encyclopedia: The UNOfficial, UNAuthorized, and UNPrecedented History of Every Land, Attraction, Restaurant, Shop, and Event in the Original Magic Kingdom Updated Second Edition (Santa Monica: Santa Monica Press LLC., 2012), pp. 288-289.

#67 Tony Baxter, Interview at The Pacific Northwest Mouse Meets (June 28, 2014).

#68 Tony Baxter, Interview at The Pacific Northwest Mouse Meets (June 28, 2014).

#69 David Koenig, Castle Drawbridge Will Never Rise Again, http://mousepad.mouseplanet.com/entry.php?1207-Castle-Drawbridge-Will-Never-Rise-Again (September 7, 2014).

#70 Disneyland History, Country Bear Playhouse Information, http://dldhistory.com/dldhistory/asp/disneyland_attraction.asp?Page=3&Ident=560&MediaType=Image (10/1/2014).

#71 Jeff Heimbuch and George Taylor, Communicore Weekly Podcast, Show #129, (7/22/2014), www.communicoreweekly.com.

#72 Disney Signs, http://disneysigns.tumblr.com/page/3 (October 9, 2014).

#73 Alice Davis, Former Walt Disney Imagineer, Interview at Be Our Guest Dinner at the Golden Vine Wine Trattoria in Disney's California Adventure, (June 10, 2013).

#74 Alice Davis, Former Walt Disney Imagineer, Interview at Walt Disney Family Museum (September 13, 2014).

#75 Merriam-Webster's Dictionary, http://www.merriam-webster.com/dictionary/esplanade (October 21, 2014).

#76 hobbyzine, Indian Head Penny Values, http://values.hobbizine.com/indian-cents.html (November 2, 2014).

#77 Chris Allison, DisGeek Podcast for pointing these out to me.

Barbara Aunt Bee Coffman, for pointing me at a web page explaining the myth:

History Myths Debunked, Myth #12: From the era of the ancient Greeks to early America, the pineapple has long been a symbol of hospitality, http://historymyths.wordpress.com/2010/07/18/myth-12-from-the-era-of-the-ancient-greeks-to-early-america-the-pineapple-has-long-been-a-symbol-of-hospitality/ (July 18, 2010).

Rod Mongenel, for pointing me at additional information about Finial:

Wikipedia, Finial, http://en.wikipedia.org/wiki/Finial (April 11, 2014).

#78 Sam Gennawey, The Disneyland Story: The Unofficial Guide to the Evolution of Walt Disney's Dream (Birmingham: Keen Communications, 2014), p. 141.

#79 Pierce, Todd J, The Truth about the Petrified Tree, http://www.disneyhistoryinstitute.com/2014/10/dhi-mythbusters-edition-truth-about.html (October 13, 2014).

Sam Gennawey, The Disneyland Story: The Unofficial Guide to the Evolution of Walt Disney's Dream (Birmingham: Keen Communications, 2014), p. 140.

#80 Ballon-Animals.com, Aliens from Toy Story (claw game), http://www.balloon-animals.com/forum/index.php?topic=3174.0;wap2 (November 7, 2014).

IMDB.com, Toy Story 2 (1999) Trivia, http://www.imdb.com/title/tt0120363/trivia (November 7, 2014). Matt Stopera, 33 Things You Probably Didn't Know About The 'Toy Story' Trilogy, http://www.buzzfeed.com/mjs538/33-things-you-probably-didnt-know-about-the-toy (February 23, 2011).

#81 zdouf.com, Things You Never Knew About Toy Story, http://www.zdouf.com/6156/things-you-never-knew-about-toy-story/ (January 10, 2014).

Jack Spence, Letter Perfect - Disney's Hollywood Studios - Part Four, http://land.allears.net/blogs/jackspence/2010/11/disney_world_lettering_part_fo.html (November 18, 2010).

#82 Disneyland, Dumbo the Flying Elephant, https://disneyland.disney.go.com/attractions/disneyland/dumbo-the-flying-elephant/ (November 8, 2014).

Disneyland, Dumbo the Flying Elephant, https://disneyland.disney.go.com/au/disneyland/dumbo-the-flying-elephant/ (November 8, 2014).

#83 davelandweb, Dumbo Flying Elephants, http://davelandweb.com/dumbo/ (11/8/2014).

#84 The Disney Wiki, Dumbo the Flying Elephant, http://disney.wikia.com/wiki/Dumbo_the_Flying_Elephant (November 8, 2014).

#85 Dave DeCaro, Sailing Through Sundays on The JC, http://davelandblog.blogspot.com/2009/06/sailing-through-sundays-on-jungle.html (6/21/2009).

#86 Jeff Kurtti, Walt Disney's Imagineering Legends and the Genesis of the Disney Theme Parks (New York: Disney Editions, 2008), p.139.

#87 The DisGeek Podcast, Show #44 We Do It Gungnam Style! (9/12/2012), www.disgeek.com

#88 Jeff Kurtti, Walt Disney's Imagineering Legends and the Genesis of the Disney Theme Parks (New York: Disney Editions, 2008), p.2.

#89 Steven M Orme, Hunting Hidden Mickeys: A Photgraphic Guide to Hidden Mickeys, (U.S.A.: Synergy Books Publishing, 2014), p. 138.

#90 Steven M Orme, Hunting Hidden Mickeys: A Photgraphic Guide to Hidden Mickeys, (U.S.A.: Synergy Books Publishing, 2014), p. 150.

#91 Dave DeCaro, Under Construction, http://davelandblog.blogspot.com/2013/05/under-construction.html (May 9, 2013).

Dave DeCaro, Mark Twain, Chicken of the Sea, and a follow-up, http://davelandblog.blogspot.com/2007/04/mark-twain-chicken-of-sea-and-follow-up.html (4/18/2007).

Dave DeCaro, Cascade Peek Construction, http://davelandblog.blogspot.com/2007_11_22_archive.html (12/16/2007).

#92 Steven M Orme, Hunting Hidden Mickeys: A Photgraphic Guide to Hidden Mickeys, (U.S.A.: Synergy Books Publishing, 2014), p. 126.

#93 Steven M Orme, Hunting Hidden Mickeys: A Photographic Guide to Hidden Mickeys, (U.S.A.: Synergy Books Publishing, 2014), p. 126.

#94 Dinah Williams, Secrets of Disneyland: Weird and Wonderful Facts about the Happiest Place on Earth, (New York: Sterling Children's Books, 2013) p. 65.

#95 Jon Ament pointed this one out to me.

#96 Kevin Yee and Jason Schultz, 101 Things You Never Knew About Disneyland: An Unauthorized Look at the Little Touches and Inside Jokes (Orlando: Zauberreich Press, 2005-2007), #59.

#97 Kevin Yee and Jason Schultz, 101 Things You Never Knew About Disneyland: An Unauthorized Look at the Little Touches and Inside Jokes (Orlando: Zauberreich Press, 2005-2007), #58.

Sam Gennawey, The Disneyland Story: The Unofficial Guide to the Evolution of Walt Disney's Dream (Birmingham: Keen Communications, 2014), p.46.

#98 David Hoffman, Little Known Facts About Well-Known Places: Disneyland (New York: Metro Books, 2008), p. 45.

#99 David Hoffman, Little Known Facts About Well-Known Places: Disneyland (New York: Metro Books, 2008), p. 83.

#100 Kevin Yee and Jason Schultz, 101 Things You Never Knew About Disneyland: An Unauthorized Look at the Little Touches and Inside Jokes (Orlando: Zauberreich Press, 2005-2007), #56.

#101 Kevin Yee and Jason Schultz, 101 Things You Never Knew About Disneyland: An Unauthorized Look at the Little Touches and Inside Jokes (Orlando: Zauberreich Press, 2005-2007), #56.

#102 Jason Surrell, Pirates of the Caribbean: From the Magic Kingdom to the Movies (New York: Disney Editions, 2005), p. 80.

#103 Jason Surrell, Pirates of the Caribbean: From the Magic Kingdom to the Movies (New York: Disney Editions, 2005), p. 71.

#104 HBG2, Jean Lafitte and the "Mega-Theme" Temptation, http://longforgottenhauntedmansion.blogspot.com/2010/09/jean-lafitte-and-mega-theme-temptation.html (September 14, 2010).

#105 The Jungle Cruise boat names are as follows:

1. Amazon Belle *
2. **Congo Queen** *
3. **Ganges Gal** *
4. **Hondo Hattie**
5. **Irrawaddy Woman** *
6. **Kissimmee Kate**

7. **Nile Princess** * +
8. Orinoco Adventuress *
9. Suwanee Lady *
10. **Ucayali Una** +
11. **Yangtze Lotus** *
12. **Zambezi Miss** *

13. Magdalena Maiden **

14. Mekong Maiden * **

* Denote opening day boat name.   ** Retired in 1997.   + Wheelchair equipped.

As part of the 2014 Jingle Cruise overlay, the boat names were changed to more festive names. The boats had the following names:

1. Jingle Belle
2. **Candy Cane Queen**
3. **Ginger-Bread Gal**
4. **Hanukkah Hattie** (sic)
5. Irrawaddy Snow Woman
6. Kissimmee under the Mistletoe

7. **Noel Princess**
8. **Navidad Adventuress**
9. Sugar Plum Lady
10. Evergreen Una
11. Yuletide Lotus
12. Peppermint Miss

The names I have been able to identify that were used in 2013 Jingle Cruise overlay were as follows:

1. Amazon Jingle Belle
2. **Congo Caroler**
3. Ganges Garland*
4. **Hondo Holly**
5. Irrawaddy Snow Woman **
6. Yule Kissimmee

7. Nile Nut Cracker
8. Orinoco Ornament
9. **Suwannee Sleigh**
10. Ucayali Egg Nog
11. **Yangtze Yuletide**
12. Zambezi Miss-Tletoe

* This boat gave the first Jingle Cruise ride.   ** Unconfirmed.

Dave DeCaro, Sailing Through Sundays on The JC: Boat Names, http://davelandblog.blogspot.com/2009/07/sailing-through-sundays-on-jc-boat.html (July 19, 2009).

Chris Strodder, The Disneyland Encyclopedia: The UNOfficial, UNAuthorized, and UNPrecedented History of Every Land, Attraction, Restaurant, Shop, and Event in the Original Magic Kingdom Updated Second Edition (Santa Monica: Santa Monica Press LLC., 2012), p. 232.

Strodder, Chris, The Disneyland Book of Lists (Solano Beach: Santa Monica Press LLC, 2015) p.117.

DisFanReview, Jingle Cruise Adds Festive Holiday Magic To The Classic Disneyland Attraction, http://www.disfanreview.com/2013/11/this-holiday-season-sees-lot-of-festive.html (November 21, 2013).

Disney and More, Disneyland "Jingle Cruise" Opening Day HD Video!, http://disneyandmore.blogspot.com/2013/11/disneyland-jingle-cruise-opening-day.html (November 12, 2013).

Disney Wikia, Jungle Cruise, http://disney.wikia.com/wiki/Jungle_Cruise (April 7, 2015).

Jason DZ, Disneyland Resort Photo Update - 11/08/13 Disneyland, http://land.allears.net/blogs/lauragilbreath/2013/11/disneyland_resort_photo_update_56.html (November 8, 2013).

MintCrocodile, Viva Christmas Time! at the Disneyland Resort, http://mintcrocodile.blogspot.com/2013/11/viva-christmas-time-at-disneyland-resort.html (November 15, 2013).

Mouse Planet, Jingle Cruise, http://www.mouseplanet.com/10550/Disneyland_Resort_Update (November 25, 2013).

samara0nvr0slps, Jingle Cruise, http://navigatingdisney.blogspot.com/2013/12/jingle-cruise.html (December 5, 2013).

thesmileoctopus, Jingle Cruise 2014: Jingle Cruise FOREVER, http://thesmileoctopus.tumblr.com/post/103615863288/capturingthejunglemonster-jingle-cruise-2014 (November 25, 2014).

A couple of great friends contributed to the holiday list.
    Michelle Young (Disney Dream Girls podcast)
    Randy Crane (Stories of the Magic podcast)

Russell Flores: I also visually verified many of the names used by the boats both during the regular season and holiday seasons.

#106 The Sweep Spot, Show #60 Walt Disney's Enchanted Tiki Room (July 28, 2012), www.thesweepspot.com.

#107 Alan Joyce, Secrets of the Mouse: An Unofficial Behind-the-Scenes Guide to Disneyland Park, (Lexington: UNK, 2008), p. 23.

#108 Sam Gennawey, The Disneyland Story: The Unofficial Guide to the Evolution of Walt Disney's Dream (Birmingham: Keen Communications, 2014), p.232.

#109 Disney Parks Blog, Then and Now: Lafitte's Anchow at Disneyland Park, http://disneyparks.disney.go.com/blog/2012/08/disneyland-park-then-and-now-lafittes-anchor/ (8/20/2012).

#110 www.hiddenmickeys.org, Hello! My name is Nancy and I am your Jungle Cruise Stripper....er, Skipper, http://www.hiddenmickeys.org/disneyland/secrets/Adventure/Jungle.html (November 14, 2014).

themickeywiki.com, Jungle Cruise, http://themickeywiki.com/index.php?title=Jungle_Cruise (February 28, 2014).

wikipedia.org, Jungle Cruise, http://en.wikipedia.org/wiki/Jungle_Cruise (October 30, 2014).

MiceChat.com, Jungle Cruise Gunshot Cheat Sheet?, http://micechat.com/forums/disneyland-resort/132694-jungle-cruise-gunshot-cheat-sheet.html (November 14, 2014).

The Disneyland Report, Guns return to Jungle Cruise boats at Disneyland (2004).

#111 Gavin Doyle, The Disney Dose Podcast, Show #DD018 Imagineer, Sculptor, Puppeteer Terri Hardin worked on Ghost Busters, Big Thunder Mountain, and the Muppets Part 1 (October 30, 2014), http://disneydose.com/ (October 30, 2014).

#112 Gavin Doyle, Disneyland Secrets (U.S.A.: UNK, 2014), p. 46.

#113 Random House, The Halloween Tree, http://www.randomhouse.com/book/17077/the-halloween-tree-by-ray-bradbury (November, 21, 2014).

#114 Jim Korkis, Walt's Friend, Ray Bradbury, http://www.mouseplanet.com/10001/Walts_Friend_Ray_Bradbury (June 7, 2012).

#115 Deb Wills, The Country Bear Jamboree Is Back -- New Shorter Version, http://land.allears.net/blogs/debwills/2012/10/the_country_bear_jamboree_is_b.html (October 18, 2012).

#116 Deb Wills, The Country Bear Jamboree Is Back -- New Shorter Version, http://land.allears.net/blogs/debwills/2012/10/the_country_bear_jamboree_is_b.html (October 18, 2012).

#117 Talk Disney, Country Bear Jamboree, http://www.talkdisney.com/forums/country-bear-jamboree.htm (September 12, 2012).

#118 The Disney Wki, The Five Bear Rugs, http://disney.wikia.com/wiki/Five_Bear_Rugs (November 26, 2014).

#119 Russell Flores: I personally confirmed that the instruments were not playing and that music was coming from the building on a trip to Disneyland November 2014.

#120 This little gem was pointed out to me by my friend Lynn Yaw in April 2013.

#121 Bob Thomas, Walt Disney: An American Original (New York: Disney Editions, 1976, 1994), p. 272.

#122 Adrienne Vincent-Phoenix, Backstage at the original Haunted Mansion pet cemetary, http://www.mouseplanet.com/10529/Backstage_at_the_original_Haunted_Mansion_pet_cemetery (October 31, 2013).

#123 Chris Strodder, The Disneyland Encyclopedia: The UNOfficial, UNAuthorized, and UNPrecedented History of Every Land, Attraction, Restaurant, Shop, and Event in the Original Magic Kingdom Updated Second Edition (Santa Monica: Santa Monica Press LLC., 2012), p. 252.

#124 Disneyland, Shops, http://disneyland.disney.go.com/shops/disneyland/ (December 12, 2014).

#125 Disneyland Inside Out, Tomorrowland, http://disneylandinsideout.com/disneyland/tomorrowland (December 12, 2014).

#126 Chris Strodder, The Disneyland Encyclopedia: The UNOfficial, UNAuthorized, and UNPrecedented History of Every Land, Attraction, Restaurant, Shop, and Event in the Original Magic Kingdom Updated Second Edition (Santa Monica: Santa Monica Press LLC., 2012), p. 423.

#127 Joshua C. Shaffer, Discovering The Magic Kingdom: An Unofficial Disneyland vacation Guide (Bloomington: AuthorHouse, 2010), p. 162.

#128 Lenny's Alice in Wonderland, FAQ, http://www.alice-in-wonderland.net/alice11.html (December 13, 2014).

Helen Thomas, What does the 10/6 label on the Mad Hatter's hat mean?, http://www.quora.com/What-does-the-10-6-label-on-the-Mad-Hatters-hat-mean (November 7, 2012).

David Hoffman, Little-Known Facts about Well-Known Places: Disneyland (New York, Metro Books, 2008), p.122.
#129 Imagineeringdisney.com, 1962 Disneyland Souvenir Map - High Res, http://www.imagineeringdisney.com/blog/2009/9/7/1962-disneyland-souvenir-map-high-res.html (September 7, 2009).

#130 Wikipedia, Disneyland Railroad, http://en.wikipedia.org/wiki/Disneyland_Railroad (Decemebr 13, 2014).

#131 Michael Broggie, Walt Disney's Railroad Story: The Small-Scale Fascination That Led to a Full-Scale Kingdom (Pasadena: Pentrex Media Group, 1997), p. 233.

Michael Campbell, President Carolwood Pacific Historical Society, email interview (December 13, 2014).

#132 Steve DeGaetano, Welcome aboard the Disneyland Railroad!: The Complete Disneyland railroad Reference Guide (Winnetka: Steam Passages Publications, 2004), p. 61.

Sam Gennawey, The Disneyland Story: The Unofficial Guide to the Evolution of Walt Disney's Dream (Birmingham: Keen Communications, 2014), p.67.

#133 Michael Broggie, Walt Disney's Railroad Story: The Small-Scale Fascination That Led to a Full-Scale Kingdom (Pasadena: Pentrex Media Group, 1997), p. 248.

#134 There are 50 boats on the Pirates of the Caribbean.

1 Amelie	11 Mathilde	21 Kimmi
2 Yvette	12 Odette	22 Constance
3 Fantine	13 Stephanie	23 Eloise
4 Josette	14 Simone	24 Colette
5 Cecile	15 Musetta	25 Josephine
6. Monique	16 Claudine	26 Christine
7 Anna Belle	17 Carolina*	27 Juliet
8 Valentina	18 Dominique	28 Gabriella
9 Calico Jack	19 Capt Mainwaring	29 Fancis Verney
10 Marietta	20 Camille	30 Giselle

31 Lisette	41 Penelope
32 Capt. Kidd	42 Muriel
33 Justine	43 Blackbeard
34 Henrietta	44 Destine
35 Fleurette	45 Jolie
36 Angelique	46 Maria
37 Eugenie	47 Mystique
38 Desiree	48 Aimee
39 Louisa	49 Sabine
40 Carlotta	50 Marianne

*All boats names were confirmed visually by the author except Carolina.

#135 Kevin Kidney, I speak for the tree, http://miehana.blogspot.com/2011/11/i-speak-for-tree.html (November 27, 2011).

MiceChat, I speak for the tree, http://micechat.com/blogs/in-the-parks/3240-disneyland-updates-dca-construction-transformers-harry-potter-news-uni.html (December 1, 2011).

#136 Gavin Doyle, Disneyland Secrets: Grand Tour of Disneyland's Hidden Details (U.S.A.: Disney Dose, 2014), p. 65).

#137 Sheila Hagen, John Hench, http://www.mouseplanet.com/6820/John_Hench (February 10, 2004).

#138 Tour at Walt's Barn conducted by Bill Barbe (April 20, 2013).

#139 Michael Campbell, Carolwood Foundation, email interview (December 13, 2014).

#140 Bob Gurr, former Imagineer, interview (December 14, 2014).

#141 Chris Strodder, The Disneyland Encyclopedia: The UNOfficial, UNAuthorized, and UNPrecedented History of Every Land, Attraction, Restaurant, Shop, and Event in the Original Magic Kingdom Updated Second Edition (Santa Monica: Santa Monica Press LLC., 2012), p. 264.

#142 Werner Weiss, Rainbow Mountain Stagecoach Ride, http://www.yesterland.com/stagecoach.html (April 25, 2008).

Dave DeCaro, All Aboard the Disneyland Stagecoach, http://davelandblog.blogspot.com/2014/02/all-aboard-disneyland-stagecoach.html (February 19, 2014).

"Matterhorn", Disneyland Stagecoaches at the Studio, http://matterhorn1959.blogspot.com/2009/10/disneyland-stagecoaches-at-studio.html (October 28, 2009).

#143 Michael Broggie, Walt Disney's Railroad Story: The Small-Scale Fascination That Led to a Full-Scale Kingdom (Pasadena: Pentrex Media Group, 1997), p. 255.

#144 Chris Strodder, The Disneyland Encyclopedia: The UNOfficial, UNAuthorized, and UNPrecedented History of Every Land, Attraction, Restaurant, Shop, and Event in the Original Magic Kingdom Updated Second Edition (Santa Monica: Santa Monica Press LLC., 2012), p. 264.

#145 Paul Reubens, better known as "Pee-Wee Herman", was the voice of REX. As a nod to Paul Reubens in the back story for the attraction, REX was manufactured by the Reubens Robotic Systems.

#146 Endor Express, RX-24, http://www.endorexpress.net/database/pilot-droids/rx-24/ (January 3, 2015).

#147 Wookieepedia, RX-24, http://starwars.wikia.com/wiki/RX-24 (January 3, 2015).

#148 Wookieepedia, Star Tours, http://starwars.wikia.com/wiki/Star_Tours_%28real-world%29 (January 3, 2015).

#149 Davelandweb, Main Street, U.S.A., http://davelandweb.com/mainstreet/ (December 28, 2014).

#150 Allears, Star Tours - The Adventures Continue Dsny's Hollywood Studios, http://allears.net/tp/mgm/star-tours-the-adventures-continue.htm (January 3, 2015).

#151 DLDHistory, Disneyland Stage Coach Information, http://dldhistory.com/dldhistory/asp/disneyland_attraction.asp?Page=3&Ident=519&Current=1&Sort=&FilterBy=&Filter=519&Action=0&PicPage=0&MediaType=&SortBy=&SortDir=&LastItem= (December 29, 2014).

#152 The names of the weasels are Smarty, Greasy, Psycho, Wheezy, and Stupid.

The Disney Wiki, Toon Patrol, http://disney.wikia.com/wiki/Toon_Patrol (January 9, 2015).

#153 Troy Taylor, Houdini! A Magician Among the Spirits, http://www.prairieghosts.com/houdini.html (January 9, 2015).

#154 Sam Gennawey, Interview (January 10, 2015).

#155 Nadyah Tayeh, Interview (October 28, 2014).

#156 Sam Gennawey, The Disneyland Story: The Unofficial Guide to the Evolution of Walt Disney's Dream (Birmingham: Keen Communications, 2014), p.70.

#157 Micechat, Mine Train Through Nature's Wonderland leftovers, http://micechat.com/forums/disneyland-resort/139473-mine-train-through-natures-wonderland-leftovers.html (June 26, 2010).

#158 In addition to listening to the recording myself, you can find a copy at this web site: Houdini Museum, Harry Houdini's Voice, https://www.youtube.com/watch?x-yt-cl=84838260&x-yt-ts=1422327029&v=D50yh3WV-OQ (November 4, 2012).

#159 Pointed out to me by my friend Lynn Yaw.

#160 Chris Strodder, The Disneyland Encyclopedia: The UNOfficial, UNAuthorized, and UNPrecedented History of Every Land, Attraction, Restaurant, Shop, and Event in the Original Magic Kingdom Updated Second Edition (Santa Monica: Santa Monica Press LLC., 2012), p. 352.

#161 Chris Strodder, The Disneyland Encyclopedia: The UNOfficial, UNAuthorized, and UNPrecedented History of Every Land, Attraction, Restaurant, Shop, and Event in the Original Magic Kingdom Updated Second Edition (Santa Monica: Santa Monica Press LLC., 2012), p. 269.

#162 Chris Allison, DisGeek Podcast, Pointed out to me on January 18, 2015.

#163 The Sweep Spot, Show #69 A Tour of Disneyland with Sam Gennawey (October 6, 2012), www.thesweepspot.com.

#164 Chris Strodder, The Disneyland Encyclopedia: The UNOfficial, UNAuthorized, and UNPrecedented History of Every Land, Attraction, Restaurant, Shop, and Event in the Original Magic Kingdom Updated Second Edition (Santa Monica: Santa Monica Press LLC., 2012), p. 232.

#165 This tree was pointed out to me by Jon and Bess Ament after they took the Disneyland Cultivating the Magic Tour.

#166 Seth Kubersky, Photo Gallery: Disneyland Cultivating the Magic Tour Part 2 (Frontierland, Fantasyland, Tomorrowland), http://blog.touringplans.com/2014/02/18/disneyland-cultivating-the-magic-tour-photos-part-2/ (February 18, 2014).

dawnredwood.org, History, http://www.dawnredwood.org/HISTORY.htm (January 28, 2015).

#167 Randy Bright, Disneyland Inside story (New York: Harry N. Abrams, Inc., 1987), p. 72.

#168 The Disney Wiki, Yeti, http://disney.wikia.com/wiki/Yeti (October 15, 2013).

davelandweb, TheMatterhorn PG 2, http://davelandweb.com/matterhorn/index2.html (January 29, 2015).

#169 The Disney Wiki, Dragon Maleficent, http://disney.wikia.com/wiki/Dragon_Maleficent (January 29, 2015).

#170 John Frost, The Disney Blog, Leave Murphy Alone (also new Fantasmic Dragon debuts at Disneyland), http://thedisneyblog.com/2009/09/02/leave-murphy-alone-also-new-fantasmic-dragon-debuts-at-disneyland/ (September 2, 2009).

The Disney Wiki, Dragon Maleficent, http://disney.wikia.com/wiki/Dragon_Maleficent (January 29, 2015).

#171 Nancy Johnson, Dis Unplugged, Orchestrion Shares its Past at Disneyland's Re-Imagined Penny Arcade - See more at: http://www.disunplugged.com/2012/05/25/orchestrion-shares-its-past-at-disneylands-re-imagined-penny-arcade/#sthash.xI1fP0Z6.dpuf (May 25, 2012).

#172 Erin Glover, Disney Parks Blog, Restoring a Piece of Disneyland History: The Main Street Arcade Orchestrion, http://disneyparks.disney.go.com/blog/2012/03/restoring-a-piece-of-disneyland-history-the-main-street-arcade-orchestrion/ (March 19, 2012).

#173 Jason Surrell, The Haunted Mansion: From Magic Kingdom to the Movies (New York: Disney Editions, 2003/2009), p. 74.

#174 Todd J. Pierce, Disney History Institute, DHI Mythbusters Edition - The Truth About The Petrified Tree, http://www.disneyhistoryinstitute.com/2014/10/dhi-mythbusters-edition-truth-about.html (October 13, 2014).

#175 Jason Surrell, The Haunted Mansion: From Magic Kingdom to the Movies (New York: Disney Editions, 2003), p. 71.

#176 The Disney Wiki, Leota Toombs, http://disney.wikia.com/wiki/Leota_Toombs (January 29, 2015).

#177 Jason Surrell, The Haunted Mansion: From Magic Kingdom to the Movies Updated 40th Anniversary edition (New York: Disney Editions, 2003/2009), p. 98.

#178 Lyndsay Gamber, 20 More Disneyland Secrets You Don't Know, http://lyndsaygamber.hubpages.com/hub/20-More-Disneyland-Secrets (July 21, 2014).

#179 Lyndsay Gamber, 20 More Disneyland Secrets You Don't Know, http://lyndsaygamber.hubpages.com/hub/20-More-Disneyland-Secrets (July 21, 2014).

findingmickey, Disneyland Hidden Disney: Secrets & Details > Frontierland > Chief Waves-A-Lot, http://findingmickey.squarespace.com/other-hidden-dl/frontierland/16980034 (January 15, 2015).

#180 Lyndsay Gamber, 20 More Disneyland Secrets You Don't Know, http://lyndsaygamber.hubpages.com/hub/20-More-Disneyland-Secrets (July 21, 2014).

#181 Lyndsay Gamber, 20 More Disneyland Secrets You Don't Know, http://lyndsaygamber.hubpages.com/hub/20-More-Disneyland-Secrets (July 21, 2014).

#182 Magical Kingdoms, Roger Rabbit's Car Toon Spin, http://www.magicalkingdoms.com/dlc/parks/dl_roger.html (January 29, 2015).

#183 Lyndsay Gamber, 20 More Disneyland Secrets You Don't Know, http://lyndsaygamber.hubpages.com/hub/20-More-Disneyland-Secrets (July 21, 2014).

#184 Secrets of Disneyland, Disneyland Secrets Mickey's Toontown (video), https://www.youtube.com/watch?v=vfGCMKDXACg (February 21, 2010).

#185 Secrets of Disneyland, Disneyland Secrets Mickey's Toontown (video), https://www.youtube.com/watch?v=vfGCMKDXACg (February 21, 2010).

#186 Secrets of Disneyland, Disneyland Secrets Mickey's Toontown (video), https://www.youtube.com/watch?v=vfGCMKDXACg (February 21, 2010).

#187 Martin Miller, Enhanced Big Thunder Mountain ride adds thrills to Disneyland favorite, http://herocomplex.latimes.com/fans/enhanced-big-thunder-mountain-ride-adds-thrills-to-a-disneyland-favorite/ (March 16, 2014).

#188 Secrets of Disneyland, Disneyland Secrets Mickey's Toontown (video), https://www.youtube.com/watch?v=vfGCMKDXACg (February 21, 2010).

#189 Hidden Mickeys, Mickey's Toontown:Roger Rabbit's CarToon Spin Fun Facts, http://www.hiddenmickeys.org/disneyland/secrets/toon/rogerrabbit.html (March 29, 2000).

#190 Secrets of Disneyland, Disneyland Secrets Mickey's Toontown (video), https://www.youtube.com/watch?v=vfGCMKDXACg (February 21, 2010).

#191 Wikipedia, Big Thunder Mountain Railroad, http://en.wikipedia.org/wiki/Big_Thunder_Mountain_Railroad (January 29, 2015).

#192 The Disney Wiki, Big Thunder Mountain Railroad, http://disney.wikia.com/wiki/Big_Thunder_Mountain_Railroad (January 29, 2015).

#193 DLDHistory, Enhanced Big Thunder Mountain Ride Adds Thrills To Disneyland Favorite, http://dldhistory.com/dldhistory/asp/disneyland_article.asp?Page=5&Ident=2838&FilterBy=Current (March 20, 2014).

#194 Chris Strodder, The Disneyland Encyclopedia: The UNOfficial, UNAuthorized, and UNPrecedented History of Every Land, Attraction, Restaurant, Shop, and Event in the Original Magic Kingdom Updated Second Edition (Santa Monica: Santa Monica Press LLC., 2012), pp. 114 / 290 / 301 / 398.

#195 Quote from The Walt Disney Family Museum, "All Aboard: A Celebration of Walt's Trains" special exhibit (January 25, 2015).

#196 Wikipedia, Disneyland Railroad, http://en.wikipedia.org/wiki/Disneyland_Railroad (January 31, 2015).

#197 "Shelby", My Year With The Mouse, Locomotive Tender Seat, http://myyearwiththemouse.com/2011/10/12/locomotive-tender-seat/ (October 12, 2011).

#198 Sam Gennawey, SamLand's Disney Adventures, TIPS: Disneyland Railroad Tender Car Ride, http://samlanddisney.blogspot.com/2009/07/tips-disneyland-railroad-tender-car.html (July 16, 2009).

#199 Bill Cotter and Bill Young, The 1964-1965 New York World's Fair: Creation and Legacy (Charleston: Arcadia Publishing, 2008), p.41.

#200 Bill Cotter and Bill Young, The 1964-1965 New York World's Fair (Charleston: Arcadia Publishing, 2013), p.73.

#201 Chris Strodder, The Disneyland Encyclopedia: The UNOfficial, UNAuthorized, and UNPrecedented History of Every Land, Attraction, Restaurant, Shop, and Event in the Original Magic Kingdom Updated Second Edition (Santa Monica: Santa Monica Press LLC., 2012), p. 348.

#202 Bill Cotter and Bill Young, The 1964-1965 New York World's Fair (Charleston: Arcadia Publishing, 2004), p.41.

#203 Urban Ghosts, Full Scale X-Wing Fighter Models… But Where's the 'Real One'?, http://www.urbanghostsmedia.com/2013/07/full-scale-x-wing-fighter-models-where-is-original-prop/ (July 17, 2013).

findingmickey.com, Disneyland Hidden Disney: Secrets & Details > Tomorrowland > Star Wars X-Wing, http://findingmickey.squarespace.com/other-hidden-dl/tomorrowland/3103358 (March 26, 2015).

#204 The Disney Wiki, Snow White's Grotto, http://disney.wikia.com/wiki/Snow_White_Grotto (February 1, 2015).

#205 Hidden Mickeys, Fanatsyland: Snow White Grotto Fun Facts, http://www.hiddenmickeys.org/disneyland/secrets/fantasy/snowwhitegrotto.html (February 1, 2015).

#206 Michelle Himmelburg, The Disney Parks Blog, How One Problem Turned into Millions of Wishes at Disneyland Park, http://disneyparks.disney.go.com/blog/2011/04/how-one-problem-turned-into-millions-of-wishes-at-disneyland-park/ (April 8, 2011).

#207 Hidden Mickeys, Fanatsyland: Snow White Grotto Fun Facts, http://www.hiddenmickeys.org/disneyland/secrets/fantasy/snowwhitegrotto.html (February 1, 2015).

#208 Michelle Himmelburg, The Disney Parks Blog, How One Problem Turned into Millions of Wishes at Disneyland Park, http://disneyparks.disney.go.com/blog/2011/04/how-one-problem-turned-into-millions-of-wishes-at-disneyland-park/ (April 8, 2011).

#209 Finding Mickey, Disneyland Hidden Disney: Secrets & Details > Tomorrowland > Star Wars X-Wing, http://findingmickey.squarespace.com/other-hidden-dl/tomorrowland/3103358 (January 30, 2015).

MiceChat, X-Wing Fighter in Tomorrowland Starcade/Star Trader, http://micechat.com/forums/disneyland-resort/159274-x-wing-fighter-tomorrowland-starcade-star-trader-2.html (March 2011).

Urban Ghosts, Full Scale X-Wing Fighter Models… But Where's the 'Real One'?, http://www.urbanghostsmedia.com/2013/07/full-scale-x-wing-fighter-models-where-is-original-prop/ (July 17, 2013).

The RPF, full scale X-Wing in progress, http://www.therpf.com/f79/full-scale-x-wing-progress-164897/ (March 22, 2013).

#210 Rolly Crump / Jeff Heimbuch, it's Kind of a Cute Story (USA, Bamboo Forest Publishing, 2012), p. 102.

#211 imnotbad.com, Exclusive Roger Rabbit Ride Designer Interview - Marcelo Vignali, http://www.imnotbad.com/2012/04/exclusive-roger-rabbit-ride-designer.html (April 21, 2012).

#212 disneytrivia.com, General search page, http://www.disneytrivia.net/search.php?searchin=question+answer&keyword=&operator=AND&catID=2&search=Search (December 28, 1999).

#213 Alan Joyce, Secrets of the Mouse: An Unofficial Behind-The-Scenes Guide to Disneyland Park, (Lexington, CreateSpace Independent Publishing Platform, 2008) p.93.

#214 Jim Korkis, Walt's Friend, Ray Bradbury, http://www.mouseplanet.com/10001/Walts_Friend_Ray_Bradbury (June 7, 2012).

#215 Chris Strodder, The Disneyland Encyclopedia: The UNOfficial, UNAuthorized, and UNPrecedented History of Every Land, Attraction, Restaurant, Shop, and Event in the Original Magic Kingdom Updated Second Edition (Santa Monica: Santa Monica Press LLC., 2012), p. 286.

#216 Chris Strodder, The Disneyland Encyclopedia: The UNOfficial, UNAuthorized, and UNPrecedented History of Every Land, Attraction, Restaurant, Shop, and Event in the Original Magic Kingdom Updated Second Edition (Santa Monica: Santa Monica Press LLC., 2012), pp. 202, 294, 327.

#217 Werner Weiss, PeopleMover - Presented by Goodyear, http://www.yesterland.com/peoplemover.html (December 14, 2010).

#218 Werner Weiss, Adventure Thru Inner Space - Presented by Monsanto, http://www.yesterland.com/innersp.html (June 17, 2010).

#219 davelandweb, Tomorrowland, http://davelandweb.com/tomorrowland/ (February 8. 2015).

#220 Davelandblog, No Place in Tomorrowland For The Past, http://davelandblog.blogspot.com/2009/09/no-place-in-tomorrowland-for-past.html (September 8, 2009).

#221 Werner Weiss, Astro-Jets, http://www.yesterland.com/astrojets.html (June 17, 2010).

#222 Chris Strodder, The Disneyland Encyclopedia: The UNOfficial, UNAuthorized, and UNPrecedented History of Every Land, Attraction, Restaurant, Shop, and Event in the Original Magic Kingdom Updated Second Edition (Santa Monica: Santa Monica Press LLC., 2012), pp. 335, 378.

#223 Major Pepperidge (gorillasdontblog), Omnibus and Monstro, October 1962, http://gorillasdontblog.blogspot.com/2014/07/omnibus-and-monstro-october-1962.html (July 1, 2014).

#224 The three shooting Galleries were as follows:

    1. Frontierland Shooting Gallery* (July 12, 1957 - present)
    2. Main Street Shooting Gallery* (July 24, 1955 - January 1962)
    3. Big Game Safari Shooting Gallery** (June 15, 1962 - January 1982)

* Used real .22 caliber rifles.   ** Used Pellet guns.

The Frontierland Shooting Gallery is the only one still operating. It has been converted to use rifles with infrared "bullets" for safety of Cast and Guests.

Note: The Frontierland Shooting Gallery and Big Game Safari Shooting Gallery had multiple names over time.

MiceChat, The history of the 4 Disneyland Shooting Galleries, http://micechat.com/forums/disneyland-resort/28122-history-4-disneyland-shooting-galleries.html (June 9, 2006).

Chris Strodder, The Disneyland Encyclopedia: The UNOfficial, UNAuthorized, and UNPrecedented History of Every Land, Attraction, Restaurant, Shop, and Event in the Original Magic Kingdom Updated Second Edition (Santa Monica: Santa Monica Press LLC., 2012), pp. 75, 183, 260.

#225 Don Morin, 2013 Pacific Northwest Mini-Mouse Meet Up Archeology Trek, Disneyland (August 8, 2013).

#226 Werner Weiss, Don DeFore's Silver Banjo Barbecue Restaurant, http://www.yesterland.com/silverbanjo.html (May 16, 2007).

#227 davelandweb, Don DeFore's Silver Banjo BBQ, http://davelandweb.com/silverbanjo/ (February 8, 2015).

#228 Kevin Yee and Jason Schultz, 101 Things You Never Knew About Disneyland: An Unauthorized Look at the Little Touches and Inside Jokes (Orlando: Zauberreich Press, 2005-2007), #10.

#229 Wendy Lefkon, ed. Walt Disney Imagineering: A Behind the Dreams Look at Making the Magic Real (New York: Hyperion, 1996) p.110.

#230 The Matterhorn has never been a side by side sitting attraction vehicle. In all its configurations, it has always been an in-line vehicle. The sign shows the parent sitting next to their child.

#231 Sam Gennawey, The Disneyland Story: The Unofficial Guide to the Evolution of Walt Disney's Dream (Birmingham: Keen Communications, 2014), p.143.

#232 Sam Gennawey, The Disneyland Story: The Unofficial Guide to the Evolution of Walt Disney's Dream (Birmingham: Keen Communications, 2014), p.143.

David Hoffman, Little-Known Facts about Well-Known Places: Disneyland (New York, Metro Books, 2008), p.156.

Kendra Trahan, Disneyland Detective: An Independent Guide to Discovering Disney's Legend, Lore, and Magic! 50th Anniversary Update, (Mission Viejo: PermaGrin Publishing, inc., 2005), p.106.

#233 vintage everyday, Pictures of Disneyland in Opening Day, July 17, 1955, http://www.vintag.es/2014/08/pictures-of-disneyland-in-opening-day.html (August 19, 2014).

#234 Werner Weiss, Fantasyland Depot - Santa Fe & Yesterland Railroad, http://www.yesterland.com/fldepot.html (February 7, 2014).

#235 Chris Strodder, The Disneyland Encyclopedia: The UNOfficial, UNAuthorized, and UNPrecedented History of Every Land, Attraction, Restaurant, Shop, and Event in the Original Magic Kingdom Updated Second Edition (Santa Monica: Santa Monica Press LLC., 2012), p. 126.

#236 jansworld.com, Welcome to my Disneyland Timeline: This third page deals with the History of the park in 1956,as Walt began to add and improve his original ideas for Disneyland, https://www.jansworld.net/DL_1956.html (February 10, 2015).

Chris Strodder, The Disneyland Encyclopedia: The UNOfficial, UNAuthorized, and UNPrecedented History of Every Land, Attraction, Restaurant, Shop, and Event in the Original Magic Kingdom Updated Second Edition (Santa Monica: Santa Monica Press LLC., 2012), p. 49.

#237 holymtn.com, The Legend of Lord Ganesha, http://www.holymtn.com/gods/ganesh.htm (February 9. 2015).

#238 kashgar.com, The Hindu God Ganesh - Who is this Elephant Headed Deity Anyway?, http://www.kashgar.com.au/articles/ganesh (2008)

#239 DLD History, House Of The Future Information, http://www.dldhistory.com/dldhistory/asp/disneyland_attraction.asp?Page=3&Ident=467&MediaType=Image (September 23, 2012).

daveland, Monsanto House of the Future, http://davelandweb.com/hof/ (March 17, 2015).

Nate Parrish, Remembering Disneyland's House Of The Future, http://micechat.com/13596-disneyland-house-of-the-future/ (October 15, 2012).

Jennifer Harbourn, How Accurate was Disneyland's Monsanto House of the Future?, http://www.themeparktourist.com/features/20120228/6109/monsanto-house-future (March 5, 2012).

#240 Chris Strodder, The Disneyland Encyclopedia: The UNOfficial, UNAuthorized, and UNPrecedented History of Every Land, Attraction, Restaurant, Shop, and Event in the Original Magic Kingdom Updated Second Edition (Santa Monica: Santa Monica Press LLC., 2012), p. 399.

#241 Steve Barrett, Big Thunder Ranch - Horseshoe (or Mule Shoe) Hidden Mickey, http://www.hiddenmickeyguy.com/catalog/disneyland/frontierland/big-thunder-ranch-horseshoe-or-mule-shoe-hidden-mickey (February 1, 2012).

#242 This one has kind of a convoluted answer, like the story line. The Caterpillar sometime referred to as the "Blue Caterpillar" or the "Hookah-Smoking Caterpillar". However, in the Disney movie, *Alice In Wonderland*, he is simply called the Caterpillar. In the original book called "Alice's Adventures in Wonderland" by Lewis Carroll, he is also just called the Caterpillar. He does get a name Tim Burton's 2010 remake of Alice in Wonderland. The Caterpillar is referred to as Absolem.

#243 The other two attractions are it's a small world and Jungle Cruise with its Jingle Jungle overlay.

it's a small world

Jingle Jungle Cruise. You can just see the list on the table to the left.

Alice in Wonderland Wikia, Absolem, http://aliceinwonderland.wikia.com/wiki/Absolem (February 17, 2015).

Lenny's Alice in Wonderland site, Caterpillar character description, http://www.alice-in-wonderland.net/school/caterpillar.html (February 17, 2015).

#244 Justin Scarred, Disneyland Secret - The oldest living thing in the park, https://www.youtube.com/watch?v=oT3cw0e6vpk (May 11, 2013).

#245 Disneyland Guru, Disneyland Fun Facts #9, http://disneylandguru.tumblr.com/page/147 (February 21, 2015).

#246 Chris Strodder, The Disneyland Encyclopedia: The UNOfficial, UNAuthorized, and UNPrecedented History of Every Land, Attraction, Restaurant, Shop, and Event in the Original Magic Kingdom Updated Second Edition (Santa Monica: Santa Monica Press LLC., 2012), p. 290.

#247 Chris Strodder, The Disneyland Encyclopedia: The UNOfficial, UNAuthorized, and UNPrecedented History of Every Land, Attraction, Restaurant, Shop, and Event in the Original Magic Kingdom Updated Second Edition (Santa Monica: Santa Monica Press LLC., 2012), pp. 288-289.

#248 Daveland web, Nature's Wonderland, http://davelandweb.com/nw/ (February 23, 2015).

#249 Martin A. Sklar, Walt Disney's Disneyland (U.S.A: Walt Disney Productions, 1969) p. 30.

#250 Jeff Heimbuch. Author / Communicore Weekly Podcast, email interview - Mr. Heimbuch learned that the windows were the original windows from a prior interview with Rolly Crump (February 24, 2015).

#251 Lynn Baron and Ken Pellman, The Sweep Spot Podcast. Mr. Baron and Mr. Pellman have mentioned several times about being able to hear the music from the wishing well all over the Park after hours.

#252 Rolly Crump / Jeff Heimbuch, it's Kind of a Cute Story (USA: Bamboo Forest Publishing, 2012), p. 102.

#253 Sara Franks-Allen, 10 Things You Didn't Know about Disney's Splash Mountain, http://thefw.com/things-you-didnt-know-about-disneys-splash-mountain/ (February 24, 2015).

Tyler Slater, Five Things You Might Have Missed in Critter Country at Disneyland Park, http://disneyparks.disney.go.com/blog/2014/07/five-things-you-might-have-missed-in-critter-country-at-disneyland-park/ (July 16, 2014).

Jumba Jookiba, Mount St. Yell'ns... or, The Only Good Thing From The 80's, http://evilgeniusguide.blogspot.com/2013/04/mount-st-yellns-or-only-good-thing-from.html (April 28, 2013).

The Disney Wiki, Country Bear Jamboree, http://disney.wikia.com/wiki/Country_Bear_Jamboree (February 22, 2015).

The Disney Wiki, Splash Mountain, http://disney.wikia.com/wiki/Splash_Mountain (March 3, 2015).

#254 Rolly Crump, More Cute Stories Volume 1: Disneyland History, Maintenance (August 6, 2013).

#255 Chris Whitten, Don't Tread on Me: The history of the Gadsden flag and how the rattlesnake became a symbol of American independence, http://www.foundingfathers.info/stories/gadsden.html (July 5, 2001).

#256 www.motherbedford.com, Union and Liberty, http://www.motherbedford.com/Flags07.htm (February 27, 2015).

National FCF Website, Historic American Flag, http://www.nationalfcf.com/history/historicamericanflags/tabid/2192/default.aspx (February 27, 2015).

#257 Pierce By Sorrow, labor day - parking (sic), http://iseemickey.blogspot.com/2008_09_01_archive.html (September 9, 2008).

Finding Mickey, Disneyland Hidden Disney: Secrets & Details > Adventureland > Jabba the Hutt - Tarzan's Treehouse Trunk, http://findingmickey.squarespace.com/other-hidden-dl/adventureland/1676675 (February 28, 2015).

Walt & Mickey's Private Club, The Jabba Tree, http://www.disneylandclub33.com/Jabba%20Tree.htm (February 28, 2015).

Adam The Woo, TheDailyWoo - 610 (3/3/14) Disneyland Jabba The Hutt, https://www.youtube.com/watch?v=TjoyDJh4Lcc (March 3, 2014).

#258 David Koenig, More Mouse Tales: A Closer Peek Backstage At Disneyland,(Irvine: Bonaventure Press, 2002) p. 50.

#259 Disney Parks Blog, Clopin's Music Box Adds to Old-World Charm of Fantasy Faire at Disneyland Park, http://disneyparks.disney.go.com/blog/2013/02/clopins-music-box-adds-to-old-world-charm-of-fantasy-faire-at-disneyland-park/ (February 26, 2013).

#260 This was pointed out to me by my wife. She noticed it one day while we were on the attraction.

#261 Justin Scarred, Five Weird Things in Fantasyland - Disneyland, https://www.youtube.com/watch?v=2HcXfCPAg0M (August 14, 2014).

#262 The Walt Disney Family Museum, A Special Barker Bird Lands at The Walt Disney Family Museum, http://www.waltdisney.org/pepe-del-presidio (March 1, 2015).

#263 Daveland, Walt Disney's Enchanted Tiki Room, http://davelandweb.com/tikiroom/ (March 1, 2015).

Tokyomagic, Fowl Stuff At Disneyland - The Enchanted Tiki Room Barker Bird, http://meettheworldinprogressland.blogspot.com/2011/02/fowl-stuff-at-disneyland-part-1-tiki.html (February 1, 2011).

Josh, Barker Bird Changes, http://disneylandreport.blogspot.com/2013/09/barker-bird-update.html (September 7, 2013).

Josh, Walt Disney's Enchanted Tiki Room 50th Anniversary, http://disneylandreport.blogspot.com/2013/07/walt-disneys-enchanted-tiki-room-50th.html (July 8, 2013).

Disneyland Guru, 1966 Tiki Room Disneyland, http://disneylandguru.tumblr.com/post/84074727383 (May 2014).

#264 findingmickey.com, Disneyland Hidden Disney: Secrets & Details > Main Street USA > Candy Kitchen - Smellitzers, http://findingmickey.squarespace.com/other-hidden-dl/main-street-usa/2738797 (August 18, 2014).

findingmickey.com, Disneyland Hidden Disney: Secrets & Details > Main Street USA > Candy Kitchen - Smellitzers, http://findingmickey.squarespace.com/other-hidden-dl/main-street-usa/2738796 (August 18, 2014).

findingmickey.com, Disneyland Hidden Disney: Secrets & Details > Main Street USA > Candy Kitchen - Smellitzers, http://findingmickey.squarespace.com/other-hidden-dl/main-street-usa/2904129 (August 18, 2014).

findingmickey.com, Disneyland Hidden Disney: Secrets & Details > Main Street USA > Candy Kitchen - Smellitzers, http://findingmickey.squarespace.com/other-hidden-dl/main-street-usa/2904130 (August 18, 2014).

Rolly Crump / Jeff Heimbuch, it's Kind of a Cute Story (USA: Bamboo Forest Publishing, 2012), p. 103.

#265 Michael Bowling, The Enchanted Tiki Room – The Magic Behind Walt Disney's Tropical Hideaway, http://www.wdwinfo.com/history/the-enchanted-tiki-room-the-magic-behind-walt-disneys-tropical-hideaway/ (January 6, 2015).

#266 Jeff Heimbuch, Enchanted by the Tiki Room: Jeff Heimbuch flocks together with tiki birds of a feather, http://www.disneydispatch.com/content/columns/the-626/2011/02-enchanted-by-the-tiki-room/ (January 21, 2011).

Disney Insider, Hurry, Hurry to Tiki Room!, http://blogs.disney.com/insider/2014/07/17/hurry-hurry-to-tiki-room/ (August 2014).

#267 Jeff Heimbuch, author / Communicore Weekly Podcast, email interview (February 14, 2015).

#268 Eric Carpenter, MR. ANAHEIM: Even Mickey needs a mailbox now and then, http://www.ocregister.com/articles/mailboxes-514669-disneyland-anaheim.html (June 26, 2013).

#269 Michael Broggie, Walt Disney's Railroad Story: The Small-Scale Fascination That Led to a Full-Scale Kingdom (Pasadena: Pentrex Media Group, 1997), p. 233.

#270 Dave Smith, Founder of The Walt Disney Achieves, email interview (March 7, 2015).

#271 Sam Gennawey, The Disneyland Story: The Unofficial Guide to the Evolution of Walt Disney's Dream (Birmingham: Keen Communications, 2014), p.61.

Jim Korkis, Eating Like Walt Disney, http://www.mouseplanet.com/9723/Eating_Like_Walt_Disney (August 31, 2011).

The Imagineers, The Imagineering Field Guide to Disneyland: An Imagineer's-Eye Tour (New York: Disney Editions, 2008), p.13.

Bob Thomas, An American Original: Walt Disney (New York: Disney Editions, 1976/1994), p.251.

John Hench, Designing Disney: Imagineering and the Art of the Show (New York: Disney Editions, 2008), p.98.

#272 David Hoffman, Little-Known Facts about Well-Known Places: Disneyland (New York: Metro Books, 2008), p.102.

#273 Kendra Trahan, Disneyland Detective: An Independent Guide to Discovering Disney's Legend, Lore, and Magic! 50th Anniversary Update, (Mission Viejo: PermaGrin Publishing, inc., 2005), p.106.

#274 Kendra Trahan, Disneyland Detective: An Independent Guide to Discovering Disney's Legend, Lore, and Magic! 50th Anniversary Update, (Mission Viejo: PermaGrin Publishing, inc., 2005), p.164.

#275 Steve DeGaetano, Welcome aboard the Disneyland Railroad!: The Complete Disneyland railroad Reference Guide (Winnetka: Steam Passeges Publications, 2004),
p. 168.

#276 Steve DeGaetano, Welcome aboard the Disneyland Railroad!: The Complete Disneyland railroad Reference Guide (Winnetka: Steam Passeges Publications, 2004),
p. 197.

#277 Michael Campbell, Carolwood Pacific Historical Society, email interview (March 18, 2015).

"Shelby", Locomotive Tender Seat, http://myyearwiththemouse.com/2011/10/12/locomotive-tender-seat/ (October 12, 2011).

#278 findingmickey.com, Disneyland Hidden Disney: Secrets & Details > Main Street USA > Coca-Cola Refreshment Corner - Red & White Bulb, http://findingmickey.squarespace.com/other-hidden-dl/main-street-usa/15106421 (August 18, 2014).

The Disney Wiki, Refreshment Corner, http://disney.wikia.com/wiki/Refreshment_Corner (March 18, 2015).

#279 Secrets of Disneyland: Weird and Wonderful Facts about the Happiest Place on Earth (New York: Sterling Children's Books, 2013), p. 84.

Disneyland Resort, Tomorrowland, https://disneyland.disney.go.com/fr/disneyland/tomorrowland/ (March 18, 2015).

#280 davelandweb.com, Central Plaza, http://davelandweb.com/centralplaza/ (March 19, 2015).

davelandweb.com, Town Square, http://davelandweb.com/townsquare/ (March 19, 2015).

davelandweb.com, Frontierland, http://davelandweb.com/frontierland/ (March 19, 2015).

davelandweb.com, Stagecoaches / Wagons, http://davelandweb.com/frontierland/stagecoach.html (March 19, 2015).

#281 Steve DeGaetano, Welcome aboard the Disneyland Railroad!: The Complete Disneyland railroad Reference Guide (Winnetka: Steam Passages Publications, 2004), p. 61.

Michael Campbell, email interview (December 13, 2014).

#282 Michael Campbell, email interview (December 13, 2014).

#283 Michael Campbell, email interview (December 13, 2014).

#284 Michael Campbell, email interview (December 13, 2014).

#285 Michael Campbell, email interview (December 13, 2014).

#286 Mary Jo Collins, John Hench's Final Tale, http://www.wdwfanzone.com/2012/05/john-henchs-final-tale/ (May 3, 2012).

Jim Korkis, Debunking Disney Stories, http://www.mouseplanet.com/10242/Debunking_Disney_Stories (February 20, 2013).

Jeff Heimbuch, email interview (March 20, 2015).

Jack Spence, Cinderella Wishing Well - Magic Kingdom, http://land.allears.net/blogs/jackspence/2009/11/cinderella_wishing_well_magic.html (November 8, 2009).

#287 Jeff Heimbuch and George Taylor during proofing and review of the book.

fc08.deviantart.net, Disney weasels besides the ones in Who Framed Roger Rabbit?, http://fc08.deviantart.net/fs71/f/2013/071/e/0/the_disney_weasel_guide_by_tymime-d2bl7so.pdf (March 21, 2015).

The Disney Wiki, Toon Patrol, http://disney.wikia.com/wiki/Toon_Patrol (March 21, 2015).

Wickedpedia: The Disney Villians Wiki, Toon Patrol, http://disneyvillains.wikia.com/wiki/Toon_Patrol (March 21, 2015).

#288 Sam Gennawey, The Disneyland Story: The Unofficial Guide to the Evolution of Walt Disney's Dream (Birmingham: Keen Communications, 2014), p.46.

#289 The Disney Wiki, it's a small world, http://disney.wikia.com/wiki/It%27s_a_Small_World (March 22, 2015).

#290 Chris Allison, DisGeek Podcast (July 18, 2014).

Hiddenmickeys.org, Disneyland DRR, http://www.hiddenmickeys.org/disneyland/secrets/general/Trains.html (June 12, 1999).

David Yeh, Tony Baxter on the Season Pass Podcast, http://www.endorexpress.net/2014/08/tony-baxter-on-the-season-pass-podcast/ (August 21, 2014).

#291 Wikipedia, Disneyland Railroad, http://en.wikipedia.org/wiki/Disneyland_Railroad (December 13, 2014).

#292 The Disney Wiki, Primeval World, http://disney.wikia.com/wiki/Primeval_World (March 24, 2015).

#293 Kevin Kidney, Direct Message interview (March 24, 2015).

#294 Holly Bartel, Three part interview on Stories of the Magic, Episode 71, 72, and 73 (November 21, 2014 to December 5, 2014).

#295 findingmickey.com, Disneyland Hidden Disney: Secrets & Details > Tomorrowland > Buzz Lightyear Astro Blasters - Imagineered Batteries, http://findingmickey.squarespace.com/other-hidden-dl/tomorrowland/15493266 (March 26, 2015).

#296 Jim Korkis, Debunking Disney Stories, http://www.mouseplanet.com/10242/Debunking_Disney_Stories (February 20, 2013).

#297 There is no question mark at the end of the *Who Framed Roger Rabbit* movie title because in the movie industry, it is considered bad luck to have a question mark in your title.
George Taylor, Communicore Weekly Podcast, show #169 (April 8, 2015)

#298 When the submarines first opened, they had a gray color scheme. The first set of names were in use from 1959 to 1984. They were:

1. Ethan Allen
2. George Washington
3. Nautilus
4. Patrick Henry
5. Seawolf
6. Skate
7. Skipjack
8. Triton

After being re-furbished into the current yellow color scheme, the names were changed. These names were used from 1985 until the submarines were closed into 1998. The names were:

1. Argonaut
2. Explorer
3. Nautilus
4. Neptune
5. Sea Star
6. Seawolf
7. Seeker
8. Triton

When the submarines were re-opened in 2007 with the new Finding Nemo theme, the colors remained the same, but some of the names were changed. The current names are:

1. Argonaut (#807)
2. Explorer (#607)
3. Mariner (#407)
4. Nautilus (#107)
5. Neptune (#707)
6. Scout (#207)
7. Seafarer (#507)
8. Voyager (#307)

Chris Strodder, The Disneyland Encyclopedia: The UNOfficial, UNAuthorized, and UNPrecedented History of Every Land, Attraction, Restaurant, Shop, and Event in the Original Magic Kingdom Updated Second Edition (Santa Monica: Santa Monica Press LLC., 2012), p. 407.

Strodder, Chris, The Disneyland Book of Lists (Solano Beach: Santa Monica Press LLC, 2015) p.117.

Russell Flores: Current names and numbers were visually confirmed by the author.

#299 Rolly Crump, It's Kind Of a Cute Story (USA: Bamboo Forest Publishing, 2012), p.83.

#300 Rolly Crump, former Imagineer, email interview (August 28, 2014).

#301 Bob Gurr, former Imagineer, email interview (May 13, 2014).

#302 Dave Smith, Founder of The Walt Disney Achieves, email interview (March 7, 2015).

#303 Kevin Kidney, Direct Message interview (March 24, 2015).

#304 Bill Butler, Garner Holt Productions, Inc., Presentation at The Walt Disney Family Museum: For The Birds - The Art, Science & Forgotten History of Walt Disney's Enchanted Tiki Room (June 20, 2014).

#305 On July 13, 2013, I counted the lights and there were 99 bulbs.

#306 Strodder, Chris, The Disneyland Book of Lists (Solano Beach: Santa Monica Press LLC, 2015) p.168.

#307 Strodder, Chris, The Disneyland Book of Lists (Solano Beach: Santa Monica Press LLC, 2015) p.122-123.

#308 Bob Thomas, Walt Disney An American Original (New York: Disney Editions, 1976 /1994) p.263.

#309 Bob Gurr, former Imagineer, interview (April 24, 2015).

#310 findingmickey.com, Disneyland Hidden Disney: Secrets & Details > Fantasyland > It's a Small World Charlie Brown!, http://findingmickey.squarespace.com/other-hidden-dl/fantasyland/2367832 (April 30, 2015.

Lyndsay Gamber, 20 More Disneyland Secrets You Don't Know, http://lyndsaygamber.hubpages.com/hub/20-More-Disneyland-Secrets (July 21, 2014).

#311 Bob Gurr, former Imagineer, interview (April 24, 2015).

Yesterdayland, The Original Carnation Ice Cream Parlor and Restaurant, http://www.yesterland.com/carnation.html (December 18, 2012).

Chris Strodder, The Disneyland Encyclopedia: The UNOfficial, UNAuthorized, and UNPrecedented History of Every Land, Attraction, Restaurant, Shop, and Event in the Original Magic Kingdom Updated Second Edition (Santa Monica: Santa Monica Press LLC., 2012), p. 95.

#312 Camp Korey, Historic Carnation Farm , http://campkorey.org/carnation (May 1, 2015).

Major Pepperidge , The Carnation Truck Lives!, http://gorillasdontblog.blogspot.com/2010/03/carnation-truck-lives.html (March 10, 2010).

Bob Gurr, former Imagineer, interview (April 24, 2015).

Elbridge Stuart, Carnation Farms, LLC, email interview (May 2, 2015).

#313 Bob Gurr, former Imagineer, interview (April 24, 2015).

Chris Strodder, The Disneyland Encyclopedia: The UNOfficial, UNAuthorized, and UNPrecedented History of Every Land, Attraction, Restaurant, Shop, and Event in the Original Magic Kingdom Updated Second Edition (Santa Monica: Santa Monica Press LLC., 2012), p. 69.

#314 Bill Scollon, The Hidden Mickeys of Disneyland (Los Angeles / New York: Disney Editions, 2015), p.54.

#315 Jason Surrell, The Haunted Mansion: From Magic Kingdom to the Movies Updated 40th Anniversary edition (New York: Disney Editions, 2003/2009), p. 17.

#316 Bill Scollon, The Hidden Mickeys of Disneyland (Los Angeles / New York: Disney Editions, 2015), p.56.

#317 Bill Scollon, The Hidden Mickeys of Disneyland (Los Angeles / New York: Disney Editions, 2015), p.49.

#318 Bill Scollon, The Hidden Mickeys of Disneyland (Los Angeles / New York: Disney Editions, 2015), p.55.

#319 Bill Scollon, The Hidden Mickeys of Disneyland (Los Angeles / New York: Disney Editions, 2015), p.16.

#320 Jeff Heimbuch, email interview (May 13, 2015).

Chef Mayhem (AKA Jeff Baham), The ravishing bride (and vanishing groom) , http://doombuggies.blogspot.com/ (November 2, 2007).

#321 Jeff Heimbuch, email interview (May 13, 2015).

BIBLIOGRAPHY
BOOKS

Alef, Daniel. Walt Disney: The Man Behind the Mouse. Kindle Edition, 2009.

American Heritage April, 1968 - Volume XIX, Number 3, What Walt wrought: The Squeak Heard round the world. United States: American Heritage Publishing Co., Inc., 1968.

Anderson, Paul F. The Davy Crockett Craze: A Look At The 1950's Phenomenon And Davy Crockett Collectables. Hillside: R & G Productions, 1996.

Baham, Jeff. An Unauthorized story of Walt Disney's Haunted Mansion. United States: Theme Park Press, 2014.

Baham, Jeff. An Unofficial History of Disney's Haunted Mansion. United States: Doombuggies.com, 2010.

Bailey, Adrian. Walt Disney's World of Fantasy. New York: Gallery Books, 1982 / 1987.

Ballard, Donald W. Disneyland Hotel: The Early Years, 1954-1959: The Little Motel in the Middle of the Orage Grove. Freemont, CA: Magical Hotel, 2011.

Ballard, Donald W. Disneyland Hotel: The Early Years, 1954-1988 (Collector's Edition Second Edition). Modesto, CA: Parks Printing, 2013.

Bancroft, Tom. Creating Characters with Personality. New York: Watson-Guptill Publications, 2006.

Bancroft, Tom. Character Mentor. Burlington, MA: Focal Press, 2013.

Barrett, Steven M. Disneyland's Hidden Mickeys: A Field Guide to Disneyland Resort's Best Kept Secrets. Bradford, CT: The Intrepid Traveler, 2009.

Barrett, Steven M. Disneyland's Hidden Mickeys: A Field Guide to Disneyland Resort's Best Kept Secrets (2nd Edition). Bradford, CT: The Intrepid Traveler, 2007.

Berger, Adam M. Every Guest Is A Hero: Disney's Theme Parks and the Magic of Mythic Storytelling. United States: Burger Creative Assocites, Inc., 2013.

Boag, Wally and Gene Sands. Wally Boag: Clown Prince of Disneyland. United States: Camphore Tree Book, 2009.

Bright, Randy. Disneyland Inside Story. New York: Harry N. Abrams, Inc., 1987.

Brighten, Homer (Edited by Didier Ghez). Life In The Mouse House: Memoir Of a Disney Story Artist. United States: Theme Park Press, 2014.

Broggie, Michael. Walt Disney's Happy Place: Celebrating Walt Disney's Centennial. United States: Disney Enterprises, Inc., 2001.

Broggie, Michael. Walt Disney's Railroad Story: The Small-Scale Fascination That Led to a Full-Scale Kingdom. Pasadena, CA: Pentrex, 1997.

Burnes, Brain And Robert W. Butler and Dan Viets. Walt Disney's Missouri: The Roots Of A creative Genius. Kansas City: Kansas City Star Books, 2002.

Burns-Clair, Pam and Don Peri. Walt Disney's First Lady of Imagineering, Harriet Burns. Marceline: Walsworth Publishing Company, 2010.

Canemaker, John. The Lost Notebook: Herman Schultheis and The Secrets of Walt Disney's Movie Magic. San Francisco: The Walt Disney Family Foundation Press ®, LLC, 2014.

Canemaker, John. Magic Color Flair: The World of Mary Blair. San Francisco: The Walt Disney Family Museum, 2014.

Canemaker, John. Walt Disney's Nine Old Men & The Art Of Animation. New York: Disney Editions, 2001.

Cline, Becky, Rob Klein, and Max Lark. D23 presents Treasures of the Walt Disney Archives. Los Angeles: Anderson, 2011.

Cosgrove, Joseph Patrick. Walt Dreamers Me. Las Vegas: Golden Additions, 2013.

Cotter, Bill. The Wonderful World of Disney Television: The Complete History. New York: Hyperion, 1997.

Crump, Rolly (as told to Jeff Heimbuch). it's kind of a cute story (sic).United States: Bamboo Forest Publishing, 2012.

DeGaetano, Steve. From Plantation to Theme Park: The Story of Disneyland Railroad Locamotive No. 5 The Ward Kimbal. Wake Forest, NC: Steam Passeges Publication, 2006.

DeGaetano, Steve. Welcome Aboard The Disneyland Railroad!: The Complete Disneyland Railroad Reference Guide. Winnetka, CA: Steam Passages Publications, 2004.

Disney Book Group. Marc Davis Walt Disney's Renaissance Man. United States: Disney Enterprises, Inc., 2014.

Disneyland: A Complete Guide to Adventureland, Tomorrowland, Fantasyland, Frontierland, Main Street, U.S.A. .United States: Walt Disney Productions, 1957.

Disneyland: Dreams, Traditions and Transitions. United States: The Walt Disney Company, 1995.

Disneyland: The First Thirty Years. United States: Walt Disney Productions, 1985.

Disneyland: Memories of a Lifetime. New York: Disney Editions, 2000.

Disneyland: The First Quarter Century. Burbank, CA: Walt Disney Productions, 1979.

Disneyland Resort: Magical Memories for a Lifetime. New York: Disney Editions, 2002.

Disneyland Resort: Remember the Moments, A Magical Souvenir. China: Disney Enterprises, Inc., 2005.

Disneyland Resort 2012: A celebration of a wish come true. United States: 2012.

Disneyland Souvenir Tickets: A Historical Look At Disneyland Tickets. Kindle Edition, 2012.

Dunham, M.L. and Lara Bergen. Disney Junior Encyclopedia of Animated Characters: Includes characters from your favorite Disney PIXAR films. New York: Disney Press, 2009.

Farber, RH. Walt Disney Saving America's Lost Generation. Kindle Edition, 2012.

Finch, Christopher. The Art of Walt Disney: From Mickey Mouse to the Magic Kingdoms. Burbank, CA: Walt Disney Productions, 1975.

Fanning, Jim. Disneyland Challenge. New York: Disney Editions, Inc., 2009.

Fanning, Jim. Disney PIXAR Finding Nemo In The Disney Theme Parks. New York: Disney Editions, 2009.

Fantasmic!. United States: The Walt Disney Company, 1992.

France, Van Arsdale. Window On Main Street: 35 Years of Creating Happiness at Disneyland Park. Nashua, NH: Laughter Publications, Inc., 1991.

Gennawey, Sam. The Disneyland Story: The Unofficial Guide to the Evolution of Walt Disney's Dream. Birmingham, AL: Keen Communications, LLC, 2014.

Gennawey, Sam. Universal vs. Disney: The Unofficial Guide to American Theme Parks' Greatest Rivalry. Birmingham, AL: Keen Communications, LLC, 2015.

Gennawey, Sam. Walt and the Promise of Progress City. United States: Ayefour Publishing, 2011.

Ghez, Didier. Disney's Grand Tour: Walt and Roy's European Vacation Summer 1935. United States: Theme Park Press, 2014.

Goldberg, Aaron H. Disney Declassified: Tales of Real Life Disney Scandals, Sex, Accidents and Deaths. San Bernardino, CA: Quaker Scribe, 2014.

Gordon, Bruce and David Mumford. Disneyland The Nickel Tour: A Postcard Journey Through 40 Years Of The Happiest Place On Earth. Santa Clarita, CA: Camphor Tree Publishers, 1995.

Gordon, Bruce and Tim O'Day. Disneyland: Then, Now, and Forever, New York: Disney Editions, Inc., 2005.

Gordon, Bruce and Tim O'Day. Disneyland: Then, Now, and Forever, New York: Disney Editions, Inc., 2008.

Grant, John. Encyclopedia of Walt Disney's Animated Characters. New York: Harper & Row Publishers, 1987.

Green, Amy Boothe and Howard E. Green. Remembering Walt: Favorite Memories of Walt Disney, New York: Disney Editions, Inc., 1999.

Gurr, Bob. Design: Just for Fun. Riverside, CA: Ape Pen Publishing, 2012.

Handke, Danny and Vanessa Hunt. Poster Art of the Disney Parks. New York: Disney Editions, 2012.

Hahn, Don. Brain Storm: Unleashing Your CReative Self. New York: Disney Editions, 2011.

Hahn, Don. The Alchemy of Animation: Making an Animated Film in the Modern Age. New York: Disney Editions, Inc., 2008.

Heimbuch, Jeff. Main Street Windows: A complete guide to Disney's whimsical tributes. United States: Orchard Hill Press, 2014.

Hench, John with Peggy Van Pelt. Designing Disney: Imagineering and the Art of the Show. New York: Disney Editions, Inc., 2008.

Hoffman, David. Little-Known FACTS about Well-Known PLACES Disneyland. New York: Metro Books, 2008.

Holliss, Richard. Walt Disney's Mickey Mouse: His Life and Times. New York: Harper & Row, Publishers, 1986.

Hollis, Richard and Brian Sibley. The Disney Studio Story. Nee York: Crown Publishers, Inc., 1988.

Jacobs, David. Disney's America on Parade: A History of the U.S.A. in a Dazzling, Fun-Filled Pageant. New York: Harry N. Abrams, Inc., 1975.

Johnson, Mindy. Tinker Bell: An Evolution. New York: Disney Editions, 2013.

Joyce, Alan. Secrets of the Mouse: An Unofficial-Behind The Scenes Guide to Disneyland Park. Lexington, KY: CreateSpace Independent Publishing Platform, 2008.

Imagineers. The Imagineering Way: Ideas to Ignite Your Creativity. New York: Disney Editions, 2003.

Iwerks, Leslie and John Kenworthy. The Hand Behind The Mouse: An intimate biography of Ub Iwerks, the man Walt Disney called "the greatest animator in the world". New York: Disney Editions, 2001.

Kaufman, J. B.. Snow White and the Seven Dwarfs: The Creation of a Classic. San Francisco: The Walt Disney Family Foundation Press ®, LLC., 2012.

Kaufman, J. B.. The Walt Disney Family Museum: The Man, The Magic, The Memories. New York: Disney Editions, 2009.

Kinney, Jack. Walt Disney and Assorted Other Charaters: An Unauthorized Account of teh Early Years at Disney's (sic). New York: Harmony Books, 1988.

Koenig, David. More Mouse Tales: A Closer Peek Backstage At Disneyland. Irvine: Bonaventure Press, 1999/2002.

Koenig, David. Mouse Tales: A Behind-The-Ears Look At Disneyland. Irvine: Bonaventure Press, 1994/1995/2006.

Koenig, David. Mouse Under Glass: Secrets of Disney Animation and Theme Parks. Irvine: Bonaventure Press, 1997/2001.

Korkis, Jim. The Book of Mouse: A Celebration of Walt Disney's Mickey Mouse. United States: Theme Park Press, 2013.

Korkis, Jim. The Vault of Walt: Unofficial, Unauthorized, Uncensored Disney Stories Never Told. United States: Ayefour Publishing, 2010.

Korkis, Jim. The Vault of Walt: Vol. 3 Even More Unofficial Disney Stories Never Told United States: Theme Park Press, 2014.

Korkis, Jim. Who's Afraid of the Song of the South? And Other Forbidden Disney Stories. United States: Theme Park Press, 2014.

Kurtti, Jeff and Bruce Gordon. The Art of Disneyland. New York: Disney Editions, 2006.

Kurtti, Jeff. Disney Dossiers: Files of Character From The Walt Disney Studios. New York: Disney Enterprises, Inc., 2006.

Kurtti, Jeff. DISNEYLAND: From Once Upon A Time To Happily Ever After. New York: Disney Editions, 2010.

Kurtti, Jeff. DISNEYLAND Through The Decades: A Photographic Celebration. New York: Disney Editions, 2010

Kurtti, Jeff. Walt Disney's Imagineering Legends and the Genesis of the Disney Theme Park. New York: Disney Editions, 2008.

Lanzarini, Lisa, ed. Disney: The Ultimate Visual Guide. New York: DK, 2002.

Lark, Max and Steven Clark. Treasures of the Walt Disney Archives: The Ronald Reagan Presidential Library & Museum Exhibition Catalog 2012 / 2013. Los Angeles: Anderson, 2012.

Lefkon, Wendy. Birnbaum's 2003 Disneyland Resort: Expert Advice from the Inside Source. New York: Disney Editions, Inc., 2003.

Lefkon, Wendy, ed. The Imagineering Field Guide to Disneyland: An Imagineer's-Eye Tour. New York: Disney Editions, Inc., 2008.

Lefkon, Wendy, ed. Walt Disney Imagineering: A Behind the Dreams Look at Making the Magic Real. New York: Hyperion, 1996.

Lesjak, David. Service with Character: The Disney Studios & World War II. United States: Theme Park Press, 2014.

Le Mon, Leslie Jane. The Disneyland Book of Secrets 2012 One Local's Unauthorized, Rapturous and Indispensable Guide to the Happiest Place on Earth. Kindle Edition, 2012.

Lindquist, Jack with Melinda J. Combs.In Service To The Mouse: My Unexpected Journey To Becoming Disneyland's First President. Orange: Chapman University Press, 2010.

Lipp, Doug. Disney U: How Disney University Develops the World's Most Engaged, Loyal, and Customer -Centric Employees. United States: McGraw Hill, 2013.

Malmberg, Melody, ed. Walt Disney Imagineering: A Behind the Dreams Look at Making MORE Magic Real. New York: Disney Editions, 2010.

Marling, Karal Ann. Behind The Magic: 50 Years of Disneyland. Dearborn, MI: Henry Ford Museum, 2004.

Marling, Karal Ann. Designing Disney's Theme Parks: The Architecture of Reassurance. New York: Flammarion, 1997.

Maltin, Leonard. The Disney Films. United States: Popular Library, 1973.

Maltin, Leonard. The Disney Films 3rd Edition. New York: Hyperion, 1995.

Maltin, Leonard. The Disney Films: author of Great Movie Shorts. New York: Bonanza Books, 1973.

Masters, Kim. The Keys To The Kingdom: How Michael Eisner Lost His Grip. New Yor: HarperCollins Publishers Inc., 2000.

Merritt, Christopher and J. Eric Lynxwiller. Knott's Preserved: From Boysenberry to Theme Park, The History of Knott's Berry Farm. Santa Monica, CA: Angel City Press, 2010.

Merritt, Russell and J.B. Kaufman. Walt in Wonderland: The Silent Films of Walt Disney. Baltimore: The John Hopkins University Press, 1993.

Mosley, Leonard. Disney's World. Lanham, MD: Scarborough House, 1990.

Norman, Floyd. Animated Life: A lifetime of tips, tricks, and stories from a Disney Legend. New Yor: Focal Press, 2013.

O'Day, Tim, Jody Revenson, Lorraine Santoli, Leonard Shannon, The Imagineers, and Wendy Lefkon, ed. Disneyland Resort: Remember the Moments, A Magical Souvenir. New York: Disney Enterprises, Inc, 2005.

O'Day, Tim, Lorraine Santoli, and Wendy Lefkon, ed. Disneyland Resort: A Pictorial Souvenir. New York: Disney Editions, 2002.

Orme, Steven M. Hunting Hidden Mickeys: A Photgraphic Guide to Hidden Mickeys (Disneyland Edition). St. George, UT: Synergy Books Publishing, 2014.

Picture Souvenir Book of Disneyland in Natural Color. New York: Disney Editions, 1955/2005.

Pierce, Meredith Lyn. Lots to do in line Disneyland: Don't miss the magic before the ride! . Bradford, CT.:The Intrepid Traveler, 2012.

Preszler, June. Walt Disney. Mankato, MN: Bridgestone Books, 2003.

Reynolds, Robert. Roller coasters, flumes & flying saucers: the story of Ed Morgan & Karl Bacon, ride inventors of the modern amusement parks. Kindle Edition, 1999.

Schickel, Richard. The Disney Version: The Life, Times, Art and Commerce of Walt Disney. New York: Simon and Schuster, 1968.

Schroeder, Russell K. Disney: The Ultimate Visual Guide. New York: DK Publishing, 2002.

Schroeder, Russell, ed. Walt Disney: His Life In Pictures. New York: Disney Press, 2009.

Scollon, Bill. The Hidden Mickeys of Disneyland. Los Angeles / New York: Disney Editions, 2015.

Selden, Bernice. The Story of Walt Disney, Maker of Magical Worlds. New York: Yearling, 1989.

Shaffer, Jashua C. Discovering the Magic Kingdom: An Unofficial Disneyland Vacation Guide. Bloomington, NJ: AuthorHouse, 2010.

Show, Charles. Walt: Backstage Adventures with Walt Disney. La Jolla: Communication Creativity, 1979.

Sklar, Marty. Dream It! Do It!: My Half-Century Creating Disney's Magic Kingdoms. New York: Disney Editions, 2013.

Sklar, Martin A. Walt Disney's Disneyland. United States: Walt Disney Productions, 1969.

Sklar, Martin A. Walt Disney's Disneyland. United States: Walt Disney Productions, 1969 (updated with material through 1975).

Smith, Dave. Disney A to Z: The Official Encyclopedia (Fourth Edition). Los Angeles New York: Disney Editions, 2015.

Smith, Dave. Disney A to Z: The Official Encyclopedia (Third Edition). New York: Disney Editions, 2006.

Smith, Dave. Disney A to Z: The Updated Official Encyclopedia. New York: Hyperion, 1996.

Smith, Dave. Disney Trivia from the Vault: Secrets Revealed and Questions Answered. New York: Disney Editions, 2012.

Smith, Dave. The Quotable Walt Disney. United States: Disney Enterprises, Inc., 2001.

Smith, Dave. Walt Disney Famous Quotes. United States: The Walt Disney Company, 1994.

Smith, Dave and Steven Clark. Disney: The First 100 Years (Updated Edition), New York: Disney Enterprises, Inc., 2002.

Smith, David W. In The Shadow of the Matterhorn. St. George, UT: Synergy Books Publishing, 2012.

Snyder, Chuck. Windows On Main Street: Discover the Real Stories of the Talented People Featured on the Windows of Main Street, U.S.A. . New York: Disney Editions, Inc., 2009.

Stewart, Whitney. Who Was Walt Disney? . New York: Penguin Group (USA), Inc., 2009.

Strodder, Chris. The Disneyland Book of Lists: The Unofficial, Unauthorized, and Unprecedented!. Solano Beach: Santa Monica Press LLC., 2015.

Strodder, Chris. The Disneyland Encyclopedia: The UNOfficial, UNAuthorized, and UNPrecedented History of Every Land, Attraction, Restaurant, Shop, and Event in the Original Magic Kingdom. Santa Monica: Santa Monica Press LLC., 2008.

Strodder, Chris. The Disneyland Encyclopedia: The UNOfficial, UNAuthorized, and UNPrecedented History of Every Land, Attraction, Restaurant, Shop, and Event in the Original Magic Kingdom (Updated Second Edition). Solano Beach: Santa Monica Press LLC., 2012.

Surrell, Jason. The Art Of The Haunted Mansion. New York: Disney Editions, 2003.

Surrell, Jason. Pirates of the Caribbean: From the Magic Kingdom to the Movies. New York: Disney Editions, Inc., 2005.

Surrell, Jason. The Disney Mountains: Imagineering at its Peak. New York: Disney Editions, Inc., 2007.

Surrell, Jason. The Haunted Mansion: From the Magic Kingdom to the Movies. New York: Disney Editions, Inc., 2003.

Surrell, Jason. The Haunted Mansion: From the Magic Kingdom to the Movies (Updated 40th Anniversary edition). New York: Disney Editions, Inc., 2009.

Susanin, Timothy S. Walt before Mickey: Disney's Early Years, 1919-1928. Jackson: University Press of Mississippi, 2011.

Sutcliffe, Jane. Walt Disney. New York: Barnes and Noble, 2009.

Thie, Carlene. A Photographer's Life with Disneyland Under Construction. Riverside, CA: Ape Pen Publishing Company, 2002.

Thie, Carlene. Disney Years: Seen Through a Photographer's Lens. Riverside, CA: Ape Pen Publishing Company, 2002.

Thie, Carlene. Disney's Early Years: Through the Eye of a Photographer. Riverside, CA: Ape Pen Publishing Company, 2002.

Thomas, Bob. Disney's Art of Animation From Mickey Mouse To Beauty and the Beast. New York: Hyperion, 1991.

Thomas, Bob. Disney's Art of Animation From Mickey Mouse To Hercules. New York: Hyperion, 1997.

Thomas, Bob. Walt Disney: An American Original. New York: Disney Editions, 1976 / 1994.

Thomas, Bob. Walt Disney: Magician of the Movies. United States: Gosset & Dunlap, Inc. & Rutledge Books, Inc., 1966.

Thomas, Frank and Ollie Johnston. The Illusion of Life Disney Animation. New York: Disney Editions, 1981.

Trahan, Kendra. Disneyland Detective: An INDEPENDENT Guide to Discovering Disney's Legend, Lore, and Magic! . Mission Viejo, CA: PermaGrin Publishing, Inc., 2005.

Van Eaton Galleries. the story of Disneyland an exhibition and sale. California:M2M PR & Partnerships, 2015.

Walt Disney's Comics and Stories: No. 688 January 2008. United States: Gemstone Publishing, 2008.

Walt Disney's Disneyland. United States: Walt Disney Company, 1993.

Walt Disney's Disneyland: A Pictorial Souvenir. United States: Walt Disney Productions, 1976.

Walt Disney's Guide to Disneyland. United States: Walt Disney Productions, 1959.

Walt Disney's Guide to Disneyland. United States: Walt Disney Productions, 1964.

Walt Disney's The Original Disneyland: Pictorial Souvenir New 1993 Edition. United States: The Walt Disney Company, 1993.

Walt Disney's Way. Kindle Edition: New Word City, 2010.

Williams, Dinah. Secrets of Disneyland: Weird and Wonderful Facts about the Happiest Place on Earth. New York: Sterling Children's Books, 2013.

Williams, Pat with Jim Denney. How to be Like Walt Disney: Capturing the Disney Magic Every Day of Your Life. Deerfield, FL: Health Communications, Inc., 2004.

Wolf, Scott and Shani Wolf. Where in Disneyland Park? . Burbank, CA: Page Publishing, 1994.

Yee, Kevin and Jason Schultz. 101 Things You Never Knew About Disneyland: An Unauthorized Look at the Little Touches and Inside Jokes. Orlando, FL: Zauberreich Press, 2005-2007.

Yee, Kevin. Walt Disney World Hidden History: Remnants of Former Attractions & other Tributes. Orlando, FL: Ultimate Orlando Press, 2010.

Zibart, Eve. Today in History: Disney. Cincinnati, OH: Emmis Books, 2006.

MAGAZINES (No specific articles were used but many magazines were reviewed)

D23

Disney Family Fun.

Disney Files Magazine.

Disney Insider

Disney Magazine.

Disney Rewards.

Disneyland Back Stage Pass.

Disneyland Resort: Annual Passholder News.

E Ticket

National Geographic

LIFE

INTERNET

Numerous Internet sites were researched in the making of this book. Please see End Notes for sites used.

MISCELLANEOUS

Miscellaneous Your Guide to Disneyland Park guide books were consulted.

Numerous videos and movies were researched in the making of this book. Please see End Notes for ones used.

DISNEY LANGUAGE

Attraction: Any ride or show.

Audio-Animatronic (AA): A robotic machine used to simulate a living person, animal or character. The movements were made by hydraulics or pneumatics which were controlled by relays. The relays were triggered by audio signals. If an AA is near or above a Guest, then the Imagineers use a pneumatics system for safety, otherwise they use a hydraulic system. (EN: 304)

Animatronic: The same in concept as Audio-Animatronics, only they're movement is created with hydrolics, pneumatics, or electrical means and are controlled by digital signals. The Digital Animation Control System (DACS) not only controls the animatronics, but controls all aspects of the show.

AP: Annual Pass.

Bad Show: Any actions by a Cast Member or other part of a Park that would cause a Guest to have a bad experience.

Back Stage: See Off Stage.

Back Story: The story of a character, attraction, or experience that explains why something is the way it is.

Cast Member (CM): An employee of The Walt Disney Company. This carries from the philosophy that Disneyland is like a multidimensional movie experience.

Costume: A Cast Members clothing

D23: The Official Disney Fan Club.

DACS: Digital Animation Control System. This computer controls all of the animatronics movements, along with lights, music, and other aspects of a show.

Dark Rides: An attraction that is entirely or mostly inside. This allows Imagineers to completely control lighting and sound.

DVC: Disney Vacation Club.

Forced Perspective: A method of designing buildings or other objects to make them appear to be taller, larger, or even smaller than they really are. On Main Street, U.S.A. the buildings are constructed so each story is slightly smaller than the lower one. This makes it appear to be much taller than it actually is.

Friends With: A Cast Member who plays a character. It allows a Cast Member to discuss being a character without destroying the magic for little ears. i.e. I'm friends with so-and-so.

Good Show: Doing a professional job and keeping Guests happy.

Guest: Most businesses refer to patrons as customers. Disney refers to its patrons as Guest to foster an attitude and feeling of how they want Cast Members to treat their patrons.

Hidden Mickey: The set of three circles that generally form the shape of a classic Mickey Mouse head. Some are obvious while others take some looking.

Imagineer: A person who works for Disney Imagineering. The are part Engineer and part artist.

Imagineering: The part of the Disney family of companies that is responsible for the designing of Disney Attractions and parks.

Meet and Greet: An event where Guests can meet, talk with, and get autographs from a character.

Multiplane Camera: A camera concept developed by Bill Garity and his staff. The camera allows the animators to place various pieces of a scene on different planes to be filmed and moved independently of each other. This allows the Disney cameramen to film a scene more realistically by moving objects that are closer to the observer faster than objects that are deeper in the scene.

Off Stage: Part of Disneyland not normally opened to Guest access.

On Stage: Any part of Disneyland that Guests have normal access.

Out Door Vending (ODV): Any outdoor location that sells food or merchandise.

Overlay: Where a theme or concept is added to an attractions regular appearance. The most commonly known overlays are the Haunted Mansion Holiday overlay for Haunted Mansion and Holiday overlay to it's a small world.

Park or The Park; A shortened reference to the Disneyland Park.

Plus, Plus It, or Plussing: When Disney re-furbishes, upgrades, adds to an attractions or in some way changes an attraction to make it more enjoyable for guests.

Plush, Plushes: When you see a cloth Disney Character or animal in one of the stores, do not refer to them as stuffed animals. Walt Disney would never stuff one of his characters. They are referred to as plush animals or characters.

Queue: A line you stand in for an attraction, food or entry/exit.

Re-furb: Short for re-furbishment.

Re-purposed: To reuse an item after it is no longer needed in its current function. The item may be used in whole or in part. It could even be modified.

Re-themed: The change the existing theme of an attraction.

Soft Opening: When Disney opens an attraction for short periods before its official opening to allow Imagineers to do final testing and adjustments, Cast Member training, ensure procedures will work properly, and a little sneak peek for Guests.

Story Board: This concept originated with Walt Disney and is now commonly used in the movie and theme park industries. A story is represented by a series of drawing showing key scenes. It allows the story artist to visualize and adjust the orders and speed of scenes. Scenes can also be easily added, moved, or removed. This book went through a story board session just prior to submission for printing to ensure the flow and pace of the book.

Streetmosphere: Characters and theming added to a part a part of the Park to give it a more realistic feeling.

Theme Phrasing: Words, phrases, or accents used by characters to make them more believable. (EN: 294)

Themed: The central idea or concept for an attraction or area.

Tooth Pick Holder: Many people see the small collector drinking glasses at Disneyland and think they are "shot" glasses. They are officially known as tooth pick holders.

Tribute: This is where an object or reference is incorporated into a new attraction to show respect for a previous attraction.

Walt Disney Imagineering (WDI): The department within the Disney family of companies that is responsible for the design and maintenance attractions found in the Parks.

WED: This was the forerunner to Walt Disney Imagineering. Originally formed from Walt Disney's staff from the Walt Disney Studio. It stands for Walter Elias Disney.

Weenie: A feature, usually large, that attracts the attention of guests and draws them closer to the attraction. There is a famous story where Walt Disney came up with the idea. One night, when he arrived home late after a long day, Walt Disney was sitting in his kitchen eating a hot dog (or wiener). He realized his dog was attracted to the wiener. This gave him the idea for the name Weenie for any device used to attract guests into a certain direction. (EN: 271)

AUTOGRAPHS